TARGET-GROUP EVANGELISM

TARGET-GROUP EVANGELISM

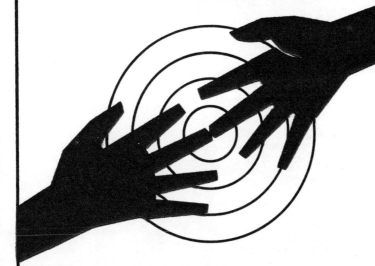

Ralph W. Neighbour, Jr. and Cal Thomas

BROADMAN PRESS
Nashville, Tennessee

4255-51
ISBN: 0-8054-5551-5

Dewey Decimal Classification Number: 248.5
Library of Congress Catalog Card Number: 74-20309
Printed in the United States of America

*Outsider, you say you can't figure out the
"Christians" in your town? You have concluded
they must play religious games inside their
expensive church buildings? They never seem
to be around where you play your games?
They're always . . . "In There?"*

*They aren't really "People Who Don't Give
a Hoot." They're scared of you! They don't
know what to say to you!*

*We're praying this book will help them learn
how to talk to you. Having been (among other
things!) skeptics, desperate, and hurting
ourselves, we know what a frustrating life
you've got now.*

*Be patient. We're pretty sure that whoever reads
these pages will finally come. People Who Care are
coming soon . . . honest!*

Foreword

Contemporary evangelism, and the evangelism of the immediate future, must be sensitive to our fragmented society. Communities are, in reality, groups or clusters of peoples within the community. Ralph Neighbour has seen this perhaps as clearly as anyone on the scene today.

Some time ago he saw the reversal of sociological pattern For generations we had operated in a "melting pot" concept That is, as people migrated to a new country, particularly America, they settled in language and ethnic groupings (ghettos). Then *assimilation* began: migrants began to dress like "American," talk like, act like, look like, and finally, to marry and rear "Americans."

Now, however, we are *regrouping!* The depersonalizing forces of our anonymous society have necessitated this regrouping. We are now reclustering around language, national, religious (and antireligious), age, and vocational patterns. One who now views a community with the idea of evangelism must see it as *groups* within the community: language groups, alcoholics, divorcees, drug addicts, golfers, attorneys, and so forth. These are what we mean by "target groups."

Churches which still operate on a general "y'all come" approach to evangelism will inevitably miss major audiences. This is especially important as we Americans squarely face the fact that only 40 percent of our population will now "come and hear" the gospel. If the 60 percent who will *not* come are to be reached, they *must* be reached "out there" in the world where they live and work and play. However, they must not be viewed *en masse*—for they are not! We must see

vii

3866775

them in the context of their *communities* within the community-at-large.

Ralph Neighbour not only saw it several years ago, he *did something about it*. His previous writings illustrate and document the story. Now, however, he generously shares with us the "how" of target-group evangelism as modeled at the West Memorial Baptist Church in Houston. We are both grateful and indebted.

Finally, Ralph Neighbour has seen clearly that the evangelism task is, in the main, the assignment of the laity. They do not have to "go" into the target group world—they are already there! The unavoidable task before contemporary Christianity is the mobilization of the laity in target-group evangelism and ministries.

There it is, then: lay-led, target-group evangelism. It represents the future . . . now!

DAVID HANEY

Contents

Introduction

A unique congregation formed to do raw research in evangelism in Houston, Texas in 1969. Dubbed "The People Who Care" locally, their official name became The West Memorial Baptist Church. Located in a sea of apartment complexes and lovely homes, the members set out to discover how to share Christ with the "Unchurchables." They deliberately ignored Christians who moved into the fast-growing area, and devoted their time instead to dialogue with those usually unreached by building-centered programs.

The story of how it all began, as well as an initial training course developed to equip others for such ministry, is now available in these earlier books:

The TOUCH of the Spirit (Broadman, 1972)

The Seven Last Words of the Church (Zondervan, 1973)

This Gift Is Mine (Broadman, 1974)

Journey into Life-style Evangelism (Baptist Brotherhood Commission, 1974)

This book is a sequel to *The TOUCH of the Spirit*, which provides a basic training for target-group evangelism. It answers the scores of questions asked by readers of that book concerning how specific TOUCH ministries are carried on.

A further report on the progress of "The People Who Care" simply reinforces the effectiveness of the TOUCH approach. The last year saw a doubling of membership, and worship services climbing to over 800 in attendance. Amazing . . . for a group who existed for over two years before any sort of a building was used by them! After proving a congregation *can* live without heavy investments in real estate, they next pioneered in the development of a shared-use building. A commercial day-care corporation rented a 10,000 square foot building from the congregation, under contract to pay all bills for 25 years. The church has access to this space evenings and weekends without charge . . . a $285,000 savings over the years!

Next, these plucky Christians erected TOUCH Center. Designed to be used "eight days a week," not a single room of this building waits for Sunday to happen. The weekday ministries there include counseling by a psychiatrist, roller skating, recreation, a coffeehouse, and much, much more. Dozens of congregations have borrowed the floor plan, also determined *not* to build another "Sunday Only" monstrosity.

Now over six years old, the life of this Body has been reported in magazines and by the Associated Press. Officials from several denominations have come to visit. "The People Who Care," however, are much more impressed by the fact they have gained the attention of the Outsiders who live about them in the Memorial Drive community! The congregation is swelling with the searching people who discovered in TOUCH groups that Jesus Christ is alive and well, in full charge of his family. From a living room full of people, hundreds now meet to celebrate the inner life in worship services.

When God called me to leave my "coaching position" to accept the Foreign Mission Board's invitation to develop house churches in Singapore, TOUCH ministries kept right on ministering effectively. As many as twenty a Sunday have come to join the pastorless flock. The ministry of the members still expands.

One of those members is Cal Thomas, formerly with NBC News (now with KPRC-TV, Houston) and the receiver of a coveted George Peabody Award for excellence in reporting. As coauthor, Cal "nosed" around the TOUCH ministries, interviewing the folks who were actually *doing* the things described in this volume. His perceptive view of the ministries has been the stuff from which I have prepared the final manuscript. It took a special kind of person to "see" TOUCH in action, and his years of covering news made by Presidents and earthquakes provided the expertise to insure "on-the-spot coverage" in each chapter. Especially dear to him was his own Thursday Morning Prayer Breakfast for men. Prominent leaders of the community were frequently among those who came at 7 A.M. to eat his wife's superb Eggs Benedict, quiche Lorraine, or, occasionally, bacon 'n eggs. Men frequently left to struggle through the day with Christ's claim of lordship.

Our nation's population is increasingly being crowded into apartments and town houses. Some forecasters feel that 80 percent of Americans will live in them by the turn of the century. This book pioneers in reporting ways to reach the people in these complexes. Until now, very little is in print to help Christians know how to TOUCH them. West Memorial's population is now primarily apartment housed . . . with a turnover averaging 110 percent, per year, per unit! We pray those faced with this "new generation" of transients will take heart from our reports of success.

This book is not _theory_, you see, but simply the "reporting in" that warm, loving Christians so often do after they have been in TOUCH with Outsiders.

You, dear reader, can also use _your_ living room, dining room, or town-house club room to reach out to others. Those who have already started to do so pray earnestly you will be inspired to join them in the most thrilling concept of evangelism known to man: Target-Group Evangelism!

Heartfelt thanks are extended to Vivian Hargrove, missionary to Togo, for her assistance in typing the manuscript and to Pat Quick, who drew the "Lovin' TOUCH" cartoons.

RALPH W. NEIGHBOUR, JR.
Ambassador for the TOUCH People

1

Glad You're Back, Fred

Come in this house, Fred! ' I thought I'd *recognize* your car when you pulled up, but you have a new one, don't you? Let's see, I haven't seen you since we took that trip together and discussed the gifts of the Spirit. Oh, take the *green* lounge chair; it's just perfect for a long conversation. The logs in the fireplace are banked to burn without attention, and there's peppermint tea in the pot on the hearth. Help yourself . . . I drink it without sugar . . . you might try it that way before "doctoring" it.

Your note indicating you would come by intrigued me. As I expected, those who discover the significance of spiritual gifts soon find a keen desire to relate to those who are outside the family of God. The need for the body to communicate more completely with those who will never come inside our church buildings is critical. I can understand why you find it disconcerting to spend so many hours in activities inside stained-glass walls and yet see so few added to the body as a result.

You wrote me about the frustration you are feeling because of the lack of relationship between your church and your community. You have every right to be concerned! An alarming number of people are now untouched by our evangelistic endeavors. Do you know that about 2 percent of the American public quits attending church every year? Actually, only 38 percent of our population still have a meaningful relationship to some church or synagogue. *Shocking, isn't it?*

I think one reason for this lack of interest is because many folks found the activities in our buildings superficial, not supernatural. Those who have not found God in mechanical services and classes that met, *met*, and *MET*, finally quit coming back. In today's rapidly secularizing society, 62 percent of our neighbors do not bother to attend any more.

Now, you and I know that the power of the Holy Spirit to call men to repentance is still as great as ever! Changed lives still validate the lordship of Christ! Scripture still has power to speak to man's needs! Why, then, should the gap between Christ and "Outsiders" be continually widening? (By "Outsiders," Fred, I'm referring to unbelievers who wouldn't be caught *dead* in a church service!)

The longer we study the problem, the clearer the answer becomes. The church has not yet provided a deliberate "go structure" to send its committed nucleus to those who have rejected our "come structures." Even when Christians *desire* to invade the world of Outsiders, *they find no structure within*

their church life to help them!

This is the critical problem. Sunday Schools and training programs, along with evangelistic services, are all buried inside church walls. Even our visitation programs and bus ministries are a part of a "come structure" mentality which seeks to "bring them *in* from the fields of sin." We do not yet possess an arm of the local church which is deliberately designed to invade the world of Outsiders.

Our structure still remains committed to what some call "circle evangelism." That is, we leave our buildings, go to the sinner, and *circle back* with him to our church buildings. There, inside the building, he will hopefully find Christ.

But Fred, 62 percent of our neighbors aren't going to *come* back with us! What happens to them? How do we reach out to share salvation's message when they won't come back? Until now, nothing of any significance has been done to reach them.

Is it not logical to create a deliberate "go structure" within the life of the local church? Ministers are desperately needed who will go . . . AND STAY . . . far beyond church walls. We might call this "arc evangelism." That is, believers go *from* the church sanctuary to *structure relationships* with Outsiders. They remain in those relationships for a long time . . . time enough for unbelievers to be exposed to the indwelling Christ. Many Outsiders will then fall in love with Christ and desire to commit their lives to him.

Sounds sensible, doesn't it? Well, then, why haven't we been doing it? For one thing, many who have seen the need for such outreach have had no *model* to follow. Humans find it easy to pattern themselves after models; when no model exists, patterns are slow in emerging. Someone had to "cut a pattern." That's why we spent five years working on a "model" in Houston!

Our first step as a congregation was to think in a new way about evangelism. Instead of always thinking, "How can we get them *in?*" we had to ask, "How can we get in to them?" We no longer desired to brag about how "we're packin' 'em in!" We began praying about how *we* could be packed *out!* A new attitude was the first step toward solving the problem, Fred.

As long as we kept kidding ourselves into thinking that a full church auditorium was proof positive that we were getting the job done, our mentality would remain committed to the antiquated "circle evangelism" methods. All the sanctuaries in town, *packed full,* could hold only a small fraction of the total population. We knew our measure of effectiveness had to be made from a new perspective.

One proposal which we considered has been used over and over by churches. It involves leaving our buildings with arms loaded with gospel tracts, to confront Outsiders with "The Way." But this is not really "sharing the good news"; it is simply providing information. A certain percentage of Outsiders (perhaps 5 percent) may be sitting at home just *waiting* for someone to tell them how to become a Christian. When an Outsider is troubled by ignorance, he will welcome one who is knowledgeable to find answers to his questions. In that situation, the sharing of tracts and a personal testimony may rapidly lead to the conversion of individuals.

But Fred, I've been working in the area of evangelism for 29 years now, and I feel I am pretty close to the truth when I say that only about 5 percent of those we approach with this method respond. That makes it valid . . . *for 5 percent!* Subtract that from the 62 percent of "unchurchables" we started with, and we have not touched the remaining. The "tract-confrontation method" is valid mainly for those troubled by ignorance.

Let me illustrate how we look to Outsiders when we use this approach:

On a recent trip through India, I flew from Delhi to Madras seated beside a Hindu businessman. We had not even gained altitude before I began to realize he intended to "evangelize" me for his faith. He zealously explained the principles upon which Hinduism is built. I recognized he was "witnessing" to me from the premise that the reason I had not become a Hindu was because I did not understand the religion. While I learned much from him, he did not bring me an inch closer to being converted. I was not troubled by my ignorance of Hinduism. Nothing in my thinking or life-style caused me to want to become a Hindu!

I say this respectfully: He undoubtedly prayed in his temple at sundown that day for my "conversion." I know he felt a warm inner glow for having shared his faith with his American friend. But nothing he did led to converting me! My survival, as I saw it, did not require my adoption of the Hindu religious system.

Why is it so hard for us to recognize that we look much the same to many Outsiders when we suddenly arrive with our tracts? Do you see, Fred, that this approach unnecessarily limits our style of evangelism? He may have needs other than being troubled by ignorance. For instance, he may be *plagued by weakness.* In that case, we can touch his life by bringing solutions to his problems . . . not information about a religious system. Or, perhaps, he is *confused about life.* A Christian who has it "together" can fill a real void for him! The key to reaching Outsiders is to discover their need and to use it to present Christ as the answer.

Another person I met on a plane trip helps to reemphasize the point. In the Denver airport I met an eighteen-year-old lad with shaved head and clad in a saffron-colored robe. As he tried to sell me Buddhist literature, I engaged him in conversation. With sinking heart, I heard him say he was an ex-Baptist. He had recently discovered in a *cult* what his *church* did not provide: a sympathetic adult who patiently listened to his problems and offered him a solution. He said to me: "I used to go to Sunday School and be drilled on

Bible history. I couldn't have cared less about dates of the kings in Israel! I was trying to get my head on straight. Nobody at church talked to me about *that* . . . but I found the *truth* from my new Buddhist teacher." You see, Fred? We had our "blinders" on to his real needs . . . and lost him to a cult! *We didn't meet his needs.*

"Arc evangelism" must function by meeting the needs of Outsiders. We must ask, "What are the *holes* in their hearts? Where do they *itch?*" . . . That's where they will welcome a *scratch.*

Fred, that's my definition of Target-Group Evangelism: *scratching people where they itch!*

As Christians meet real needs in Outsider's lives, they will be *welcomed* as friends. Many needs are common to whole groups of Outsiders. An anthropologist friend of mine says, "People differ *widely,* but not *wildly.*" So . . . divorcees have common needs, and evangelistic cell groups can be formed to discuss them. Parents of retarded children have needs that can be met by a fellowship formed especially for the purpose. Teenagers who ride motorcycles could be reached by a Christian mechanic who would be willing to open his garage one night a week for a course in repairs . . . with Bible study at the close!

The list of potential target groups is endless, Fred! Later on, after Ruth serves us lunch, Cal Thomas is going to join us, and we'll give you a *ton* of ideas to take home. I hope you'll explain to your body how these ministries function. You see, we now have a *target group model* to follow, thanks to those in Houston who worked out the "bugs" for other congregations like yours!

I'd like to recommend you call your target groups *TOUCH Groups.* At first, this word will have no meaning to people. *That's what makes the word valuable.* Since the objective of target-group evangelism is to relate Christians to Outsiders, it's important not to scare them off with words like "church,"

"Baptist," "Methodist." You see such words carry different meanings to different people. For example, I have met many men in taverns who automatically think only "antiliquor" when someone says "Baptist." Others connect the word only with "hellfire and brimstone preaching," "don't believe in dancing." Why cut ourselves off from Outsiders who have a prejudice toward what they *think* we represent by using words which cause them to reject us?

Since I was born in a Baptist parsonage, the word "Baptist" means to *me* "salvation by grace through faith," "a family of baptized believers," "love and concern." As the Outsider's day of salvation draws near, he begins to see a *new* meaning to words like "Baptist" and "church" . . . but at the start, we found it much wiser to call our target groups by a neutral word. TOUCH is a good one! It stands for "Transforming Others Under Christ's Hand."[2] To the Outsider community, TOUCH will gradually come to mean "people who care, without strings attached."

The longer you minister outside church walls under that name, Fred, the more impact it will have! Experience has validated that after strong relationships have been developed, authentic meanings of our "old words" are gradually accepted . . . and Outsiders come *inside*. In the meantime, the need for an initial breakthrough to Outsiders make TOUCH necessary.

Think of TOUCH as a *ministry*, not a program. TOUCH ministries are a form of evangelism which always occurs outside church walls. It takes place in the den of a home, an apartment club house, even in a tavern (as we shall see). Its purpose is not for the evangelization of people who *will* come to church, but for those who *won't*.

Target-Group ministries differ from traditional church evangelistic methods in three ways. *First*, the impact of Christ dwelling in the believer becomes the focal point for witnessing, rather than simply the distribution of tracts and the sharing of canned, memorized speeches. Therefore, *this type of evangelism demands the use of spirit-led believers. Second,* TOUCH ministries frequently involve the utilization of small groups, rather than using a one-to-one ministry. *Third,* TOUCH ministries utilize a cultivative approach in which believers and unbelievers share a relationship for many weeks. It does not concentrate on a quick-visit approach, which usually shorts out the opportunity to discern were Outsider's "itch" is.

If the name of a local church is not used, how do TOUCH ministries remain church related? . . . in the same way that a Sunday School class relates to a local church! TOUCH is a ministry of men and women who are commissioned by the local congregation to become ministers of Christ in the greater community of unreached persons. The church sponsors, directs, subsidizes, and receives reports from each TOUCH ministry.

Examples of TOUCH ministries currently in use include Divorcee Care Groups, a house fellowship for parents of retarded children, a ministry to Internationals who are taught to speak English, a ministry to alcoholics, a ministry to campers at a trailer park, TOUCH Clubs for children in apartment complexes, Teenage Rap-ins, a TOUCH hot line, a sharing ministry for grade school boys featuring athletics and Bible study, providing shots to diabetics and people with allergies, and a ministry conducted by men who visit bars, gas stations, and the like. It must be emphasized that in each of these situations the deliberate purpose of the group is to share Christ with Outsiders. The ratio of Christians to non-Christians in groups is always approximately one believer to every five unbelievers.

Fred, the people in your church who care may structure other TOUCH opportunities of a quite different nature. Since people do not vary *wildly,* the suggestions I'll give you will be helpful in determining how many possibilities for ministry are appropriate for your area. With every new target group you TOUCH, you will discover additional people who have been *waiting* for you to come to them with the message of Christ!

---

[1] If you haven't met Fred before, you missed *This Gift Is Mine* (Broadman, 1974).
[2] This subject is covered in depth in *The TOUCH of the Spirit* (Broadman, 1972).

2

How to Get Flowing

You're absolutely right, Fred, when you observe that Christians will need patient training before they will move into target-group evangelism. Many churches have discovered that the toughest part of all is the initial "breakout." We seem to be *most* afraid of something we are doing for the first time. This training must be slow enough for basic attitudes about the Christian life and evangelism to be altered. Anticipate the use of a year or more to involve people permanently in new outreach ministries. This time span will help you to avoid the frustration otherwise caused by impatience. People change slowly!

Fortunately, there are many materials to help you. There are also many ways this training can occur . . . including the wise use of retreats. At the end of our visit together, remind me to give you a suggested one-year strategy and a list of books and tapes you can use in helping fellow believers move into TOUCH ministries.[1]

You'll find there are two stages to launching TOUCH ministries:

FIRST, THERE WILL BE A JOURNEY INWARD

Being must come before *doing.* Once the Christian discerns his full relationship with his Lord, it will be quite natural for him to desire to be a channel for the outflowing of "rivers of living water."

Time will be an important ingredient. This is because teaching involves not only the imparting of information but also the observation of others demonstrating the principles.

24

This is what Paul had in mind when he wrote to young Timothy, "But you, my son, have followed, step by step, my teaching and my manner of life, my resolution, my faith, patience, and spirit of love, and my fortitude under persecutions and sufferings" (2 Tim. 3:10, NEB [2]). Paul recognized that the Christian life must be *observed* to be understood. The interchange between those who *have* discovered the importance of instant obedience to Christ and those who *have not* will cause maturity to begin.

Therefore, the Journey Inward will require more than teaching and preaching sessions. It will involve a *relationship between believers.* Small groups, formed for the specific purpose of taking the journey, should be seeded with some who have already moved forward in the pilgrimage. The impact of their "manner of life" will make the Word become flesh.

In recent days, an exciting way of getting a congregation moving ahead has spread across our land. I'm referring to Lay Renewal Weekends. They simply cross-pollinate "turned-on" Christians with those who have not had much opportunity to relate to deeply committed believers in action. Many a sterile church has been set aflame by the sincere sharing of other Christians during a weekend like this. If you can schedule one for your body, it will go far toward getting the Journey Inward under way.

Someone has said: "Spiritually, we shall be exactly as we now are in another five years, except for the people we meet and the books we read." That is so true! Therefore, the Journey Inward needs to insert *both* ingredients into the lives of your fellowship . . . people and books.

As the preparation within yourselves develops, five significant items should be covered. Let me summarize them for you:

1. *The one source of assurance.*—It is dangerous to provide a wrong criteria about how one is *sure* he is a Christian! First John 3:9 and 4:13 (NEB) provide the keys to understand

the foundation for assurance: "The divine seed remains in him" and "He has imparted his Spirit to us." I know I am a Christian because I know his life stirring within me. The proof of my conversion is that I begin to act, react, love, look, and respond to the events of life in a way that is more than I can explain on the basis of what my personality would do. In the same way that a woman is assured she is pregnant when she feels the constant motion of the child within her womb, even so every authentic Christian is aware of the movement of the "Divine Seed" within the life. Oh, how marvellous it is to observe this principle proving itself as valid in new converts!

2. *The two natures of the believer.*—Practically every baby Christian goes through a "honeymoon period" following conversion. For a few weeks, he lives in the glow of his new relationship with Christ. Old habits may be sluffed off, a thirst for the Scripture develops, and he is filled with joy. Then, the honeymoon stops.

A man may find his lust is not dead. A woman finds her old depressions returning. A teenager discovers his old habits are just as strong as ever. Disillusionment sets in. "It won't work for me!" may become the attitude of a young believer. I have discovered that often the convert is *ashamed* to verbalize this to anyone, and this makes the problem twice as hard for him to live with. It is almost as though any admission of the problem would be to "let God down."

Fred, you may intercept many members of the fellowship in your inward journey *who stopped growing years ago* . . . at this precise point! Feeling that they aren't authentic in their own Christian life, they will be extremely hesitant to be exposed to the honesty of TOUCH ministries.

David Tryon's booklet *Always at War* suggests this outline which we have often used to cover the topic: [3]

(1) The lusts of the flesh are not to be overcome by negative suppression, but by positive counteraction (Gal.

5:16).

(2) The lusts of the flesh are not overcome by one great jump but by a steady walk (Gal. 5:25).

(3) The lusts of the flesh are overcome by a walk in the Spirit (Eph. 5:18).

3. *The three aspects of salvation.* —Next, your groups will want to understand that salvation is first *a point in time*, followed by *a process in time*, with a *concluding point in time*. At a *point* in time we are saved from the *penalty* of sin. Next, as a *process*, we are continually saved from the *power* of sin. Finally, at a *point* in time *yet future* for all living Christians, we are to be saved from the *presence* of sin. Understanding that the act of becoming a Christian is only the *beginning end* of the Christian life, and that growth will then occur, is basic to doctrinal foundations concerning salvation.

When this is not understood, there is additional confusion about what God does at the beginning end of salvation and what he does in the years which follow. To understand that the power of the "old nature" is broken in the life of the obedient believer is the key to growth, Fred. It is here that Paul admonishes us to "work out [our] salvation with fear and trembling." Forever set free from the *penalty* of sin, continually being set free from the *power* of sin, looking forward to the day . . . either at death or the rapture . . . when we are set free from the *presence* of sin.

4. *The four possible sources of religious authority.* —Fred, I have often diagrammed these on the back of an envelope in the midst of a discussion group! I draw two lines dividing the paper into four parts. The two parts on the *left* are titled, "Outside Sources"; the two on the *right*, "Inside Sources." *Outside*, the sources for religious authority are: (1) The Institution—when the "church" speaks, the truth has been handed down; (2) The Scripture—hopefully, we will discover this to be supreme for each one in the fellowship! *Inside*, the possible sources are (1) The Intellect—what is not reasonable to me

is not true; (2) The Experience—I shall not question what I have "felt inside!"

Each Christian must face the fact that many possible combinations of these authorities will be found in working with Outsiders. *Which authority is authentic?* I firmly believe that there is only one primary authority we can use for the discovery of divine truth: *Scripture.* Once a believer thinks through this matter, he will develop a love for the Word that is beautiful to behold . . . and is protected from the plethora of experience-oriented religious systems which flood our world.

5. *The nature of the church and its gifts.* —The divine collection of believers at the time of their conversions into Bodies is an awesome truth! The further recognition that every single member of the Body has been given spiritual gifts for the purpose of serving the Head leads to a clear awareness that *every Christian is a minister*, and is called forth to serve him in specific ways. The role of *servant* is Christ's role for the church in the world; *this does not become authentic until each member of the body is serving.* This theological truth is so very, very clear in the New Testament, and the honest recognition of it by a congregation will leave no honest alternative but to become involved in target-group evangelism. The other four items previously mentioned buttress this final truth. We are not to wait until we become "holy men" before becoming servants in the world. Perfection of some super level is not a prerequisite for witnessing. Each child of God is *already* (despite his imperfections!) capable of "seeing the kingdom of God" . . . something that is impossible to those who have not yet been "born again." There is *no excuse* for withdrawing from ministry! It is the very focus of the body activity.

Forgive me for harping on the point, Fred, but to get these facts firmly planted in the lives of an existing church will take *t—i—m—e!* Don't try to rush the process. Six months may be about right for some and six *years* more appropriate for others! At any rate, following the suggestions I'll give you, watch for the time to . . .

SECOND, BEGIN THE JOURNEY OUTWARD

You may be surprised at what I suggest at this point: don't begin any sort of training program just yet; rather, *literally* take a "journey outward." Just now, your purpose will not be to evangelize but to *see* the world around you. Do a lot of listening and looking. Remember that every community or area has two "lives" . . . the "day life" and the "night life." Often there are two distinct groups of people in the same area simply as the result of the sun going down. An example of this may be a local custard stand which serves working men at noon and is flooded with teenagers at night. What are the *needs* of the people in your locality? Divide the area into *age groups, emotional groups, economic groups,* and others as needed. Visit local taverns and listen. Do the same in restaurants, bowling alleys, gasoline stations. Where do people go on weekends? What do they do while Christians are in Sunday School?

Ask questions. You might decide to take a survey of *religious attitudes* of those in your community. (Keep your seat belt fastened. You'll find *that* journey will jar your very *teeth!*)

What do Outsiders think of your church? One question you might innocently ask at the gasoline station closest to your church building is, "Where is the _____ Church located?" If I were a betting man, I'd lay you three moldy fig newtons *the man you ask won't know!*

Talk to teenagers. Ask them what *they* think about Jesus Christ; about the churches of the community. Sit on the curbstone and ask the grade school children at the playground where they play on Sunday morning . . . and if they have ever learned John 3:16 by heart.

Secure permission to "ride shotgun" with a policeman on

his tour of your area. Talk to the Narcotics Division about the drug problem in your area. Attend an Alcoholics Anonymous meeting. Visit with prisoners in your local jail. Spend a night in the waiting room of your county hospital's emergency ward. Find out where the local houses of prostitution are located. Spend an hour in the pool hall . . . the dance hall . . . the record shop, which also sells the accoutrements for smoking pot. Sit in the mall and visit with the "long hairs." Spend a couple of hours in the local park. Talk to the men who run the newsstands with hard-core pornography.

Chat with the waitresses at the all-night diner. Don't forget the folks at the posh country club. Ask the counselor at the high school about the pregnancy problem and the rate of dropouts. Talk to the doctors and lawyers of the community. Spend a Saturday night "across the tracks" . . . and don't leave before midnight!

This is absolutely the most dangerous thing you will be asked to do, Fred, in taking the Journey Outward. *Dangerous*—because you will never, never again be content to return to the old "business-as-usual" attitude concerning church life! The beginning of vision for TOUCH ministries is seeing the Outsiders.

Now, you're ready for some preparation to minister specifically to those hurting people you have seen. Again, the schedule I'll give you at the close of our time together (see Appendix) will help you structure this. Take another six months! Don't get anxious . . . "flash programs" fizzle. Plant roots so they will grow deep into the life-style of the body.

Continue to emphasize the value of small-group relationship to Outsiders. It is important to realize that long-term relationships outside the church walls occur in groups. Two Christians and six Outsiders can spend months in sharing situations if they are properly structured. That cell of eight people will so fill the time of the two Christians with ministry that they will wonder how they ever *could* have believed the world would be reached by ten-minute visits!

Gradually, the members of the body will move into TOUCH ministries. It may take a few weeks—even months—before the harvest appears. Remember: even a *cotton* crop requires time to grow. Give your seed-sowing and cultivation of the gospel time to mature. Let me tell you from our own personal experience that once the pattern of TOUCH ministries has been established, there is a constant harvest into the fellowship of the church.

I well recall a time at West Memorial when we had about 400 members of our fellowship, with a large percentage of them involved in TOUCH ministries. At the time, we had two morning services and had a full house on Sunday night. I really chewed my nails (I'm kidding!) during the seemingly endless months it took for TOUCH Center to be erected. *We were in a race against TOUCH time!* It was inevitable that soon . . . *very soon* . . . the Outsiders in TOUCH ministries would become the INSIDERS. We were literally reaching scores and scores of people who were not yet attending our services on Sunday. The landslide actually began before the building was finished, and we were compelled to worship in a half-finished building. Once the groundswell began, even my resignation as pastor to serve in Singapore did not slow down the influx of people.

Don't be alarmed at the time invested in launching the ministries. A farmer isn't worried about the weeks that elapse during the "growing season." Remember the Scripture that promises that those who go forth sowing precious seed will return, *bringing their sheaves with them?* That *comma* in the sentence represents . . . T-I-M-E.

Fred, here's a suggestion you'll appreciate as you actually launch the most relevant TOUCH ministries for the needs in your community: schedule the first TOUCH groups for *ten weeks,* and use *one and one-half hours* for each group meeting. Divide the time as in Figure A:

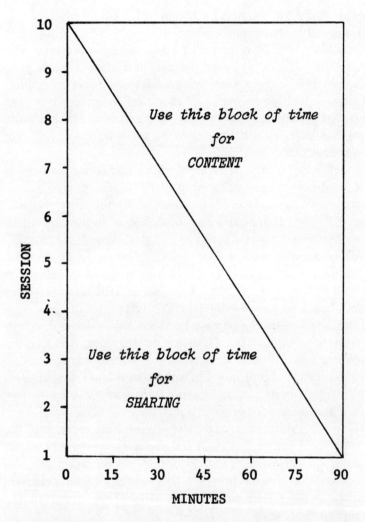

Figure A.   Division of time during ten weeks
of TOUCH Ministry Group Meetings.

The division of the time by the triangles gives an approximate use for the hour and a half in each group meeting. This does not have to be binding right down to the *minute*, of course, but it is wise to follow the suggestion. It takes about four weeks to develop a strong feeling of acceptance and trust within a group meeting together for the first time. Therefore, a majority of the early meetings should emphasize the type of sharing that will permit people to grow into each other

An excellent "opener" for many groups are the Quaker Questions [4] followed by an explanation of group sessions to follow. Additional suggestions for these fellowship times will be found in the excellent series of volumes edited by J. William Pfeiffer and John E. Jones entitled *A Handbook of Structured Experiences for Human Relations Training.*

Let me give you a copy of my book, *The TOUCH of the Spirit.* It contains the "basic training" for TOUCH ministries You will want to study it carefully. The actual structure of some TOUCH ministries will be the focal point of our time together after lunch. First, however, the basics should be digested from my earlier book.

Say! There's Cal now. Fred, after I introduce you to him, I'll tell my *stakar sliten flicka* we're ready for her Swedish spaghetti. We'll take the afternoon to fill you in on the details we learned in the TOUCH School of Hard Knocks!

See Appendix.

[2] Scripture quotations marked NEB are from *The New English Bible.* The Delegates of the Oxford University Press, and the Syndics of the Cambridge University Press, 1961, 1970. Reprinted by permission.

[3] *Always at War.* Available from Africa Evangelical Fellowship, P.O. Box 109, Glen Ridge, N. J. 07028.

[4] The Quaker Questions are: (1) Where did you live between the ages of seven and twelve, and how many brothers and sisters were at home? (2) How did you heat your house? (3) Which person was the "warmest" person in your life? (4) When did God become more than a word to you?

3
How Symbols Speak

While you eat, gentlemen, let me make a few important comments about the importance of symbols. A few years ago, I waded through Korean mud until I was far beyond the protection of the missionary compound. My camera was poised to photograph the people of the village . . . and I spoke not one word of the Korean language!

Three hours later I returned to my English-speaking friends tired but excited. I had developed several new friendships with Korean men, women, and little children.

I had used and had observed the use of a unique language; a simple and beautiful communication which men have used since the beginning of history. It is a language in which outward, visible actions reveal the inner, invisible feelings of persons. *I had communicated in the language of symbols.*

What *word* can express human love as powerfully as the caress of a hand or the light of eyes sparkling within a smiling face? Can pain ever be verbalized in greater manner than a contorted face or sorrow than through a single, lone tear rolling down a trembling cheek?

These are examples of the *universal language of symbols.* According to a dictionary, symbols are "things that stand for or represent something else; an emblem; a sign."

We live in a world of them! For example, I drove a rented auto through Switzerland and Germany, unable to speak a word of French or German. In eight hours of driving, I could not understand a single word written on a sign . . . but I never scratched a fender. But *symbols* in the form of international road markers safely guided our way.

There is, of course, a technical difference between a *sign* and a *symbol*. A sign *represents* something, takes its character from it. For example, the cross represents Christ's crucifixion in most parts of the world . . . but in Haiti it has become for many a *symbol* instead of a *sign*. There it has become a "hex sign" to ward off evil spirits. It is so used by thousands of voodoo religionists who have no idea of its Christian source. A symbol *resembles;* it has acquired a deeper meaning than the sign. It is more completely identified with the concept behind it. For example, the *sign* of the fish became a *symbol* to early Christians representing far more than the disciples who fished. It represented the very theology of Christ! The letters ICTHUS in Greek became the initial letters of the five words, "Jesus Christ, God's Son; Savior."

Sometimes symbols continue to be propagated by people who are unaware that their original meaning has been lost . . . or changed . . . by the viewers. Take church steeples, for instance. To many Americans they are symbols that cry out, "I tower over a building reserved for the Pious. Atheists, alcoholics, and adulterers are *unwelcome.*" Crosses hanging on golden chains around thousands of necks today have no connection at all with the bloody sacrifice of Christ. The "peace" symbol represents not *peace,* but drugs, free sex, and radical politics to thousands of people who tie it instead to the life-style of the bearers rather than the "cause."

As a result of this understanding of the universal language of symbols, the word TOUCH and its bird-and-heart symbol were prayerfully developed for target-group ministries. The bird: *a dove* . . . symbol of the Holy Spirit; *a heart:* symbol of the human spirit. Combined, dove above heart, the symbol speaks of the Holy Spirit in man's spirit.

It's a brand-new symbol, to be shared with the community by means of pins on lapels, stickers on cash registers, and so forth. *Being* new, it represents things which old symbols no longer say.

Ed Beck, pastor of the Warren United Methodist Church in Denver, has indicated one important value of the use of symbols in evangelism. City Manager Norm Hickey in Daytona Beach, Florida, being aware that the college set would flood the beaches in his area during Easter holidays in the 1960's, sent out an SOS to the Methodist National Board of Evangelism. In cooperation with all churches of the community, the Board selected a symbol which would clarify the message of Christ. They selected a symbol not usually used by the church (at that time) and one which would be given character because of its association with witnessing Christians. They settled on the use of the word ICTHUS and the sign of the fish. It was a natural symbol for a *beach* ministry, and had no prior meaning to college students. It was worn displayed on both pins and shirts by scores in the "Icthus Caravans" which roved the beach.

Dr. David Stewart, psychiatrist from Louisville, Kentucky, quietly observed the life of the college students on the beach. He discovered that the *primary* symbol at the beginning of the week was the *empty beer can!* As the fish appeared, he noted that the mood of the students began to change. Discussions switched from "How to make whoopee" to, "What does the fish represent? What significance does it have for us?" The change in the attitudes of the students came not from people preaching, but from the impact of the symbol and the people who wore it!

As a result, the symbol created an awareness within "pagan" students which led them to ask questions. Those who answered interpreted the fish symbol from their own background of Christian life . . . and a powerful witness was placed within thousands of lives.

Today the use of the fish is widespread—*and commonplace.* It still represents a level of Christian commitment to thousands. Fascinating! A forgotten ancient symbol was resurrected to speak once more to a new generation.

Fred, a church which begins target-group evangelism to reach Outsiders hangs a millstone around its own neck if it tries to do so using shopworn words like "revival meetings," and so forth. Why not adopt the TOUCH word *and symbol*, permitting its fresh image to reach the unreached? Experience proves it will provoke questions which committed Christians are ready and willing to answer! (Permission is granted to use this symbol. In color, the dove is always white, the heart, bright red.)

4

The Night People TOUCH Ministry

Fred, being born in a Baptist parsonage was not really the best "background" for getting involved in TOUCHing men in beer joints. During a student pastorate in New Orleans, Louisiana, the Lord began to bother me about the matter of reaching into these places. My small part-time church was located on a boulevard with at least twenty beer joints for neighbors. I deliberately began to eat lunch in some of them and gradually got to know their owners on a first-name basis.

You know, the great gulf fixed between us was more *my* attitude toward *them* than their attitude toward me. I needed that break-through during seminary days, but I had not yet learned how to hate sin and still love sinners. As a result, the response to my Lord by those tavern owners was *zero.*

While serving with the Evangelism Division of the Baptist Convention of Texas, I began to honestly face a serious problem in my life: *I did not have as many as five intimate friends among Outsiders.* As a result, I decided to leave the Baptist Building a little early each night and visit the nearby Sportsman's Lounge. For a time I just ordered colas and *listened!* Many hours were spent in this "schoolroom." Through listening I discovered this important truth: *40 percent of all discussion in taverns concerns GOD!*

I developed a first-name relationship with employees and regular customers. As they learned I was a "Professional Christian," invariably they would ask, "What are *you* doing in a place like *this?*" I learned to respond, "Let me ask *you* a question: If I did not come here, would I ever get to meet you inside a church building?"

That would usually lead them to give me a discourse about "all the hypocrites in the church." They would explain that while they might be liquor drinkers, at *least* they were not "putting on a *front* by going to church!"

I began to ask myself *why* I heard this same retort over and over again. Did they not realize that thousands of people who attended churches were *not* hypocrites?

In a word, *no!*

I think the reason they feel all Christians are hypocrites is twofold:

1. *This attitude is a part of the flight pattern of Outsiders.* Frustration leads to anxiety and that in turn leads to "the world is rotten; everyone is a hypocrite" attitude.[1]

2. *Many times the only Christians the Outsiders get to know in a personal way are the hypocrites.*

. . . The rest of us never go near them! We are too busy with our religious structures to share life with them. Did not our Lord Jesus Christ set a pattern for us all by having a reputation of being "a friend of winebibbers and sinners"? If we Christians are insulated by the Holy Spirit, there is absolutely no reason for being isolated from the nasty world of Outsiders. (Ducks have no problem living on the water in which fish swim; they do not avoid water because fish are trapped under its surface!) Dietrich Bonhoeffer scored a point when he wrote, "Only in the midst of the world does Christ become Christ."

If you agree with these statements, you may be led to begin a ministry to the Night People. Spiritual gifts which equip you for this outreach may include the gifts of wisdom, knowledge, faith, helps, and ministry, coupled to a large amount of the highest gift: LOVE.

Step by step, here's how to get started:

1. **Be called to this ministry by the Holy Spirit.** Find at least one other person who has also completed the TOUCH Basic Training to work with you.

2. **Enlist prayer support.** Share your concern with fellow Christians who have experience in intercessory prayer. I have watched several teams fizzle out, and I am convinced it was because they skipped this point.

3. **Order and prepare needed materials.** In Houston, we purchased nylon jackets imprinted with the TOUCH symbol (see Appendix). Always wear an identifying jacket when on the Night Ministry. It will soon identify you in each place you visit. The questions about the meaning of the symbol will give conversation starters with many people.

In addition, prepare TOUCH stickers similar to the one reproduced here:

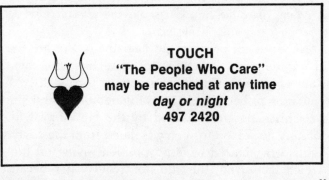

You will also want to have a local printer prepare calling cards similar to this one:

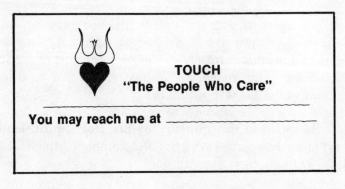

We also recommend that you order *The Way* magazine to be used as a TOUCH point in conversations. This is the most unique magazine in print today for cultivating Outsiders. It is purposely written to speak (not preach!) to Outsiders, and it is published monthly. This provides a new, changing piece of literature to share. Once one copy has been read, friends will be delighted to receive subsequent copies.[2]

You'll also find situations in which you will want to give away a booklet which clearly explains the claims of Christ and the way one receives him. The important thing is to use one which does not contain the name of any particular denominational group, which could "kill" its impact for some.

4. **Set up a "night beat" for each team.** Select the proper night or nights, and times during the night, to visit. This will vary from area to area! Sometimes a Friday evening is good. In Dallas, the downtown area was crowded from 4 to 6 P.M., but desolate later on. In Houston, our Night People ministry usually met for prayer at 8:30 P.M. on Friday evenings, and men would go out on their "beats" from 9:00 P.M. to midnight.

Each team of men should be given specific places to visit. For example, one of our teams was assigned the territory "from Dairy Ashford Road to West Belt Drive on Memorial Drive." Experience will soon let you know how many places one team can visit in one evening. It is better to have too large an assigned area at the beginning than one too small.

5. **Visit all places of business available at this time of night.** Gasoline stations, drive-in groceries, restaurants, stores, taverns, pool halls, you name it, should be visited. Quite frequently people who work in the evenings have time to visit and talk about Christ between "rushes." Young people hang around gasoline stations and restaurants. After a week or two, each team will discover the best time to visit each place.

6. Use an approach like the following at the start.

"Good evening. My name is _____. (Present the TOUCH calling card with name and telephone number written on it.) I am a volunteer worker attached to the TOUCH group in the community. Have you ever heard of TOUCH?"

"Well, we are an organization of concerned Christians who feel very strongly that we should be involved in helping people with crisis needs. We are not out to get people to join a given church, nor do we come to argue about which religion is right. Instead, we want to be known as people who care for those who may have little or no faith as well as the deeply religious. Our main purpose is to provide assistance to folks who have a need or who would just like someone to 'unload on' . . . without any strings attached to the conversation."

Additional comments may explain that teams of men will be returning at this time of evening on a regular basis. It should be indicated, in a bar especially, that when teams enter they will do so as paying customers (ordering a cola or a sandwich), and in no way will "buttonhole" people who do not desire to talk.

When entering a tavern for the first time, go to the end of the bar where the cash register is located and ask to see the manager. Quite often this will be a woman in her middle forties, divorced, with no college education. She is running the place for the owner or a syndicate of men. She does so because she can make two to three times more money than she could as a clerk or a stenographer. We frequently found these women to be very lonely, often hating their job.

Explain clearly why the team will be coming to the bar. Emphasize that they will not try to solicit conversation *or money* (many church groups regularly make the rounds of taverns for donations!), but would like to become a resource for the manager to use when people with problems need help. Present the sticker, with a request that it be placed in the cash register so the number can be found during the week when TOUCH services might be needed. Examples of situations which would be typical would include a man who is having marital problems and comes in to get drunk (bartenders don't like drunks!), a person trying to drown sorrow after the death of a loved one, one who has just been fired.

Later on, after the friendship with the manager has been established, you will be able to request that a sticker be placed in a public place: on the cash register, mirrors in rest rooms. You will be surprised at the many contacts this will generate for future ministry.

The tavern is obviously not the place for long discussions about the pros and cons of drinking liquor. Usually those who bring up this subject by asking you, "What do you think about drinking?" can best be answered with: "What do *you* think about it?" Or, sometimes I have said, "You seem to be expressing some doubt about the value of drinking. Do you sometimes feel that there is an empty place in your life which needs to be filled with something?" It is important to demonstrate a great deal of love and patience and to avoid being drawn into arguments. The best way to answer a question is with a question. It is more valuable to be quiet and to listen than to try to "hard sell" either employees or customers using logic and Scripture verses. You *could* be asked to leave and not come back . . . defeating the long-term gains of the ministry.

7. **Build a "case load" of Outsiders.** The purpose for going out on the Night People ministry is to make significant contacts with *five* Outsiders who would not be TOUCHED in any other way. When the Christian makes positive contact with five people who can be cultivated in places other than a bar or in the other establishments, he should "drop out" temporarily from the Friday night visitation and begin to utilize his available time for the cultivation of these new

friends. He may be able to establish a Bible study for them on Sunday morning in the back room of a restaurant or his own home. There may follow a time of "social contacts" between couples so met, leading to some long talks about Christ's lordship over life. Exactly *how* one proceeds with these five contacts will be an extremely individual matter, and cannot be scheduled in advance.

At a later time when the TOUCH person has need for additional Outsiders to be cultivated, he may once again return to his "route," or periodically return to it to keep in touch with those he has met. As for me, Fred, I have never felt at home in a tavern, nor have I ever really desired to spend time in one. However, those who develop a TOUCH Night People ministry will discover a large group of people, complete with aching voids within, are to be readily met in these places.

8. **Cultivate on the basis of the "Hole in the Heart."** A meaningful friendship makes openness and sharing easy between two people. This may take a month or more, but once the "phatic" communication has been developed, it will be easy to invite these new friends into your home for a barbecue, to go hunting together, etc. Cultivate on the basis of fellowship which does not compromise your own Christian testimony. Use these preliminary times of deepening the friendship to introduce your friend to as many of your own Christian friends as possible. As a result of these occasions, the men you have met will become aware that there *is* "another world," even as Paul promised there would be!

9. **Keep in personal contact on a regular basis.** Use the telephone and lunch dates to deepen the level of sharing. Remember that when your friend comes to Christ, his whole life-style will change! There is a true "culture shock" for a convert from the Outsider world. He needs to be surrounded by a loving community of Christians who will accept him exactly as he is at each step of spiritual growth.

One final comment . . .

Some men have weaknesses in their lives which make it wise for them to stay away from taverns. If a man has a history of alcoholism or feels that his being subjected to this environment might be a great temptation, he should not be encouraged to participate in this ministry. In *all* situations, the use of *teams* will be a good policy to follow.

---

[1] See *The TOUCH of the Spirit*, p. 71.

[2] Order directly from *The Way* Magazine, 2850 Kalamazoo, S.E., Grand Rapids, Michigan 49508. Sample copies available upon request.

5

Addicts Need TOUCHing, Too!

Fred, Cal and I are loading you down with more ideas than you will ever use for TOUCH ministries! Your notes will be helpful to many others when you get home, won't they?

Let me ask you to take a break while I answer the front door. I think you'll want to meet this dear friend of mine. Dr. Ernest J. Gregory has just come over from his home in San Antonio in his truck. Truck . . . that's right! This beloved physician who recently received the coveted Servant of Christ Award from the Christian Medical Society takes frequent trips into the heart of Mexico. For hundreds of peasants there, his skilled hands are the only ones they have ever known. While he is here, I want him to tell you about the TOUCH ministry to heroin addicts he has directed in San Antonio for several years. Take careful notes as he shares from his wealth of experience . . .

Well! So you're the Fred Ralph has told me about! I'm always ready to share our information about addiction. It has been a large part of my own life, since the TOUCH Narcotic Rehabilitation Ministry began.

The leading cause of death in New York City for youths between the ages of fifteen and twenty-five is overdose of heroin; it even surpasses accidents. This creeping epidemic is touching every phase of our lives, and none of us is immune to its effects.

Abuse of drugs has been recorded since 2700 B.C. when the Chinese Emperor Shen Neng recommended marijuana for gout, constipation, and absentmindedness. Opium was first used by the Egyptians around 1500 B.C. From this point its use increased, and the Europeans began to use it for cough, diarrhea, and even hysteria. Its abuse is probably first mentioned by Homer about 900 B.C. in the *Odyssey*. He called it "a drug potent against pain and quarrels and charged with forgetfulness of all trouble. Whoever drank this mingled in the bowl, not a tear would he let fall the whole day long, not if mother and father should die, not if they should slay a brother or a dear son before his face and he should see it with his own eyes."

By the eighteenth century opium was used in the United States as a pain reliever, for venereal disease, cancer, gall stones, dysentery, typhus, as a topical agent on the stomach for cramps, and on the cheek for relief of toothache. Addiction was present but not well appreciated until after the compounding of morphine (1805) and codeine (1832). These were even used to cure the opium habit. The spread of addiction was further compounded by the invention of the hypodermic needle (1843) which was used widely during the Civil War addicting hundreds of soldiers.

Other opium derivatives—such as laudanum (one grain of opium to 25 drops of alcohol), paregoric (one grain to 480 drops), and Dover's powder (opium mixed with ipecac and milk sugar)—were produced, along with their tendency for abuse and addiction. Smoking of opium was practiced mostly on the Barbary Coast by Chinese after the California Gold Rush. Pulverized opium was used in suppository form.

The final link in the opiate chain came in 1898 when heroin was synthesized. Again, it was used as primary treatment for morphine addiction with disastrous results.

Until the beginning of the twentieth century, the medical world disagreed on what "opium disease" was. It was generally felt to be no worse than gin or whiskey drinking; however, because there were no laws regulating its use, addiction was widespread and cut across all classes of society. Professional people, literary men, people with nervous disorders, society ladies, and people from all walks of life had fallen beneath the witching power of "morphia." Prominent people such as Edgar Allen Poe, Francis Thompson, Samuel Coleridge, Thomas de Quincy (the author of *Confessions of an English Opium-Eater*), John Randolph (American statesman), and the great English philanthropist and abolitionist, William Wilberforce, did not escape its clutches.

Public reaction came to the front around 1901 when a raging controversy began over whether addiction was an illness or a vice. In 1909 a law was passed which prohibited the importation of opium except for medical purposes. The law was not rigidly enforced, and the Harrison Narcotic Act was passed by Congress in 1914. This law was to regulate and control production, manufacture, and distribution of narcotic drugs, allowing only physicians to dispense narcotics, and pharmacists to dispense only by prescription. Communication between law enforcement and the medical community broke down. Doctors became frustrated in trying to treat addicts and quit dealing with them. Attempts by the government at establishing outpatient and inpatient treatment clinics in 1919 and 1932 failed.

At this point, addicts turned to the underworld for their supply. A close link between organized crime and addiction became fixed and exists to the present day.

Federal hospitals at Lexington, Kentucky, and Fort Worth, Texas, were established in 1929. Changing patterns of addiction and the widespread use by teenagers and younger youth produced the Drug Control Acts of 1956. Before the international treaties, vigorous law enforcement, and expanded drug abuse education, there were an estimated 782,000 narcotic addicts in the United States. By 1950 the estimated number had dropped to 60,000; however the epidemic has now spread rapidly, and there probably are one million addicts in the United States at the present time.

This gives us an overview of the problem nationally, but let us come closer to home. The police department of San

Antonio estimates that 80 percent of the crime in this city is related to heroin addiction. Approximately 25 percent of the heroin in the United States is now from Mexico, and much of this comes through San Antonio making this city a distribution point for all parts of the nation. We personally know of people from Florida who come to San Antonio to get their supply. It is estimated that there are 5,000 hard-core heroin addicts in our city, crossing all social, racial, and cultural barriers. Heroin can be easily obtained in all high schools and many junior high schools.

It is common knowledge that addiction has undesirable features both to society and to the addict. Crime, divorce, nonsupport of families, and total dependence on outside help for support are but a few of the social problems. Personally, the addict is subject to prison, suicide, overdose, and a myriad of physical ailments common to injection of unknown quantities of contaminated material into the bloodstream. What, if anything, can be done about it?

In October of 1968 another physician and myself were working in a Christian Medical Society outpatient clinic in San Antonio and began to be confronted with numbers of heroin addicts wanting help. The other physician felt sorry for them and began giving them methadone by prescription.

On several occasions during his absence, I would fill in. This gave me an opportunity to get to know them and to share with them what I felt Christ could do in their lives. I found them quite receptive, and gradually my interest became more intense. Pressure from the Narcotics Bureau caused my fellow physician to drop back into a consulting role, leaving our clinic director and me with several addicts depending on us for help.

After I went to the medical library for up-to-date information and communicated with local law enforcement officials, narcotics officers, and finally the Federal Drug Administration, our TOUCH program began. A scientific protocol was written and an I.N.D. number obtained. Through trial and error, after mistakes and changes, we now have our present TOUCH Narcotic Rehabilitation program operating actively in San Antonio. The laws for operating a methadone program are strict and constantly changing.

The TOUCH program is a Christian, nondenominational rehabilitation activity, utilizing methadone for the relief of the physical symptoms of heroin withdrawal, and spiritual and psychological group and individual counseling for the elimination of the psychological desire for drugs.

The objectives are accomplished by a disciplined program involving two or three meetings per week, daily methadone dispensing, Bible study, and a gradual reduction of methadone until the patient is no longer on narcotics. The patients are required to work or go to school, to attend meetings on time or face punishment, and to refrain from shooting heroin.

Our staff consists of a consulting psychologist, a consulting physician (specialist in obstetrics and gynecology), a full-time secretary, a director and assistant director, along with two medical students actively engaged in all phases of the program, and six volunteer counselors who meet with the addicts at least once a week. We usually have 20 to 35 addicts under treatment at one time.

Admission consists of a physical exam, medical history, narcotic history, Minnesota Multi-Phasic Inventory, and a battery of laboratory tests, including chest X-ray, VDRL, chemistry profile, CBC, and routine urinalysis. Addicts are required to pay $15 for this initial work-up. The addict is then placed in an orientation class and is told what is expected of him and what will be required for him to become drug free. He is then scheduled for classes on Sunday morning, Sunday night, and one night during the week. The entire program is oriented toward the spiritual Christian approach to life, and the Bible is used as a textbook. It is interesting to see addicts walking down the street carrying a Bible.

The addict's urine is tested for narcotics, and he is started on methadone. Our starting level is 30 to 60 mg. We never go any higher. We do not let the addict determine his dose, anymore than we would let a patient tell us how much penicillin we should give him. Whining and complaining is not tolerated. Gradually the dose of methadone is reduced, usually 5 mg. every two weeks. Very little physical effect is felt from this gradual drop. When the addict reaches 20 mg., we usually stop the reduction until he has progressed enough in his rehabilitation to want to be drug free. Then he is withdrawn completely. Very little physical problem is encountered. Depression is the main psychopathology, and this is treated by counseling and occasionally with antidepressants. Pregnant addicts and youth under eighteen are not treated by this program at the present time. Urine is tested twice a week for narcotics, cocaine, amphetamines, barbiturates, and quinine. The addict pays $5 a week to be on the program, an important part of the therapy since all of the men and women have jobs. If they are not working, they may do work around the center for their $5. There are employers who are willing to hire addicts as long as they are in a program, and we are able to place many of them in jobs.

Characteristics of an Addict

It would not be difficult to fill a book with the characteristics of the heroin addict, but I will try to summarize. When on the streets, the addict has one thought constantly in his mind: "What must I do to obtain my next 'fix'?" This involves "conning" his family and friends, stealing from family and friends, stealing from others, shoplifting, car prowling, burglary, selling heroin, and on rare occasions acts of violence to obtain money or goods to sell. Fences pay 10-15 percent of the actual value, so an addict usually has to steal $200 worth of goods to maintain a $30 a day habit, the average cost to our addicts. Females almost always prostitute to maintain their habit. Socially, the addict lives around addicts, goes to parties with addicts, sometimes is married to an addict, works on a job with addicts, and has very little interchange with the "clean" world. This compounds the problem of rehabilitation.

Psychologically, an addict is emotionally immature, has psychopathic tendencies, has a very low frustration level and poor ego, considers himself a failure, will not face reality, is chronically depressed, and is ambivalent toward his habit. These clinical impressions have been reflected in the Minnesota Multi-Phasic Inventory. Many of us feel that the addict has been arrested psychologically at the age he started his addiction. Almost all of our addicts have been in jail many times, some to prison two to four times, and many are on parole or on probation. They are frequently stopped and jailed for vagrancy or any other excuse that can be thought up. This increases the antagonism toward society and toward the law which is already well developed in the addict. Many are awaiting trial on charges that are one or two years old. This is an unpleasant sword hanging over their heads.

What is the spiritual condition of the average addict we see? Most come to us with absolutely no knowledge of the Bible, no spiritual awareness, have never been to church, and are atheists in action if not in philosophy. A number have come to us because we have spiritual counseling. Others turn us off at first. One or two have professed that they came to know Christ in earlier years, but were turned away early and have had no contact with any church in years.

The Addict's Wife

The addict's wife presents an interesting study and plays an important part in the rehabilitation of the addict. Her attitude and behavior are quite similar to that of the alcoholic's wife. She has become accustomed to running the household, guiding the children, making the living, and having her own way—treating her addict husband as a naughty child, feeling superior and a very necessary part of his life. When the husband starts to rehabilitate and grow as a person, she becomes insecure and resents not having her own way. Although many times it is subconscious, she pushes him back on the streets by nagging, threats of divorce, running off, and even *asking* him to go back on the streets. Often the wife will wait out a prison term of three to five years, being true to him, and then leave him when he comes home and asserts authority and assumes the dominant role. It is common for the wife to divorce one addict and then marry another.

The TOUCH program is set up with all of these factors in mind. We believe the addict needs total rehabilitation—physical, psychological, and spiritual. This takes time, possibly six months to two or three years at our present state of knowledge, particularly on an outpatient basis. He must learn to say no to early offers of heroin, and to attack the problem with hope.

Three Decisions Required

We believe that the process of rehabilitation requires three decisions on the part of the addict. In these commitments, we feel, lies the success or failure of this approach.

The first commitment is to the program. All programs have found this essential. This means not shooting heroin (violation is punished by suspension of one week if confessed and two weeks if unconfessed). The rules are irritating because an addict is not used to abiding by any rules, but a willingness to submit is the first step to progress.

The second commitment is to Christ. The conversion experience is a documented psychological fact and a spiritual necessity. The addict must experience the fact that God loves him in spite of himself and his feeling of being unwanted. He then becomes part of a community of brothers in Christ and finds a genuine fellowship with other addicts and the staff. He learns that his salvation is God's gift to him, and he doesn't have to earn it and can't lose it by slipping back to heroin. This gives him a sense of security. He learns to pray and finds that God answers his prayers. He finds that the Bible comes alive to him gradually, and he gets strength and insights into himself and what God has promised him. He develops hope not only in eternity but in this life. These factors come slowly for most, but as the staff patiently works with them, they grow. The addict becomes interested in helping his friends, and frequently prayers are heard for buddies on the streets.

The third commitment is to being drug free. This has to come as a decision of the will and usually is a culmination of spiritual and psychological growth of many months and a feeling of confidence in the future. This means leaving methadone at a low dose and going on their own. Only a few have reached this plateau so far, and the work from here is new territory. We have many drug free to our knowledge, living in the community, working regularly, and acting as responsible citizens. It is too soon to tell the final results.

The follow-up needs to be strengthened. We are training our program graduates to staff the clinic as counselors. More careful follow-up needs to be done; more intense spiritual commitment is needed; more prayer support, more knowledge of the physical, psychological, and spiritual nature of addiction, and more people dedicated to helping are necessities. It takes untold patience, a bit of courage, a great deal of stubbornness, and a faith in God's hand and leadership to work with this problem.

We claim no instant success; we claim no real expertise, but rather a minimal amount of skill in dealing with the problem; but we still feel a mandate from God to be involved.

We also believe that when a basic defect is found in the human machine, the answer will be found by going to the Designer and Creator.

Well, Fred, what do you think about that? I have met few physicians in my life who were as totally yielded to Christ as Dr. Gregory! It's awesome to realize that all this ministry to addicts is a spare-time TOUCH ministry for him . . . carried on alongside his busy medical schedule. Kind of makes you a bit ashamed, doesn't it, at the weak excuse of so many folks that "they don't have time *for target-group evangelism"? I'm convinced that we always find time for the things we consider to be important. It's a pity that Outsiders are so unimportant to so many of us. Just as soon as we care . . .* they're there . . . waiting.

6
H.O.P.E.
for unTOUCHed Internationals

English is probably the most universally spoken language in the world today. That's good . . . for Americans! They can move around the earth with comparative ease, finding someone nearly anywhere to talk to them in their native tongue.

Fred, have you ever contrasted that with the problems of Internationals who must live for extended periods in the United States? What happens to a Japanese woman in an American shopping center who does not know one word of English? What are *her* chances of meeting an American who has learned the complicated *katagana-hiragana-kanji* of the Japanese? *She's trapped!*

Her brilliant husband usually has already learned our language and is busily caught up with an embassy schedule or in a major industry. Faced with overwhelming personal adjustments in his fast-moving business world, he often has neither the time nor the energy to help his wife adjust to her new environment.

Even *color* television has no charm when you cannot understand English. How do you shop in the strange supermarkets where unknown foods are sold . . . and how do you cook them when you get home? *Trapped . . . in the United States of America!* Does anyone care about the plight of these women?

Fred, we have found dozens of such women living all around us. They have come from Asia, Europe, the Indian Subcontinent, South America, from all over the world! Some of their husbands are key men in the governments of their countries.

They needed H.O.P.E.: a TOUCH way to *Help Others Practice English*. It's a ministry designed to help women who would like to learn English and make friends with People Who Care.

The spiritual *gift of helps* will be needed for this ministry. Christians who simply *love* will find HELP a way to become trans-cultural missionaries without ever crossing the ocean. After close relationships have been established, a time naturally comes when the story of Jesus and his cross can be shared.

For example, one of our ladies had been working with a Hindu woman for many weeks, teaching English, showing her how to shop and cook, and just *caring*. One Tuesday morning as they sat down for the English lesson, the lovely mother from India said, "Why you do this? Why you take time for me?" With great tenderness, the TOUCH worker shared her own conversion experience and related how Jesus Christ had given her a new love for others. This became the turning point in the Hindu woman's understanding of Christianity.

It's easier than you might think to make contact with Internationals. Colleges and universities are good sources of information about this unique community. Students from abroad will often know about fellow nationals living in the area. If you live in or near a major city, you might find consulates will provide assistance. In fact, a consulate employee can serve as your translator as you communicate your HOPE invitations. Another possibility is to look for special sections of stores or delicatessens which sell foreign groceries. We had one HOPE student prepare a sign in Japanese for one of these establishments advertising our literacy program. The manager permitted us to tack it on the counter right next to the section where Japanese foodstuffs were stacked.

Once you have made contact, your news about ministry will travel quickly through the International community.

After the first couple of families from one country settle in
a certain apartment complex, later arrivals usually also cluster
there. The women automatically come to HOPE then . . .
it's a part of their adjustment to this new land!

Baby-sitting must be provided. It's *fascinating* to watch a
group of children playing together, speaking a total of five
or six different languages. Somehow, they seem to communicate in a special "kid language" all their own!

Here's a typical format for one of our HOPE mornings:

9:30 A.M. Meet for coffee, tea, and sweet rolls. This is an
informal time for visiting. Many will naturally
drift from the living room to the kitchen.

10:00 A.M. Introduce new students, visitors, new teachers.
Make any necessary announcements. Share any
"good news" about the families represented in
the group.

10:10 A.M. Devotional period. Read a few Bible verses (*Good
News For Modern Man* can be presented as a gift
to each student by her teacher). Verses should
be read slowly, with careful enunciation. A very,
very simple explanation should follow. Visual
materials are valuable. Flannelgraph stories are
a great way to connect words with stories. All
devotionals should be kept on a junior high
level—or under—because of the language barrier.
Remember that this is probably the first time in
their lives these ladies have ever heard these
stories!

10:30 A.M. Break into teacher-pupil pairs for the study of
the English lesson.[1] If you are short of teachers,
it works well to group two or three ladies together
from the same country. This allows shy ladies
to benefit from others who will ask questions
about the material.

11:30 A.M. Dismiss.

At least once a quarter, a luncheon should follow the HOPE session. Each lady is invited to bring a special dish typical of food in her country. American women cook their "specialties." These feasts are enjoyed by everyone, and the fellowship is tremendous.

When a lady leaves the group to return to her country, she is presented with a "HOPE Dish." A local ceramics hobbyist prepared these for us, painting the name of each woman and the word "HOPE" on it. Ladies would also be given *bushels and bushels of love* to take home! Every woman who has had to say farewell has wept openly. Frequently the only Americans she has been able to relate to were our TOUCH ladies.

Times for farewells are perfect reasons for scheduling luncheons. By the time such events take place, the group will be very close; the farewell presentations will be unforgettable experiences for all.

One young wife from Indonesia spent a year in our HOPE group. While friendly, the staff felt she could not break through her stiff formality. Finally, she opened up to her teacher: she and her husband had been the victims of some rather cruel discrimination within the community. The one bright spot in her life had been the HOPE group, where unconditional love and acceptance had been reflected. She was relieved when the time came for her husband to return to Indonesia . . . but she cried openly as she went around the room, kissing each woman farewell!

The spiritual harvest from such gatherings is often slow in comi·ig. Seed must be sown and then cultivated before results are seen. Some women return to their own nations with a new faith in Christ, but others leave still pondering the "new religion" of Americans. We have frequently given names of HOPE Internationals to missionaries in countries where the women live. We have also given women the addresses of English-speaking churches in their countries (available from foreign mission boards). Quite often they have regularly attended such services to keep up their proficiency in our language.

Expect shyness! You will find it necessary to put each woman at ease, and experience will demonstrate the best ways to do this. Warmth and love from *eyes* that say, "I accept you without reservation," mean much.

TOUCH women will do well to spend some time reading about the countries the women in their group come from. Visiting with missionaries on furlough, and talking to other Americans who have lived in their countries is also helpful.

Understanding the culture from which a woman comes is most important. Our "make a buck and buy things" attitude is *not* the attitude of all other cultures! Frequently women who come from cultures where courtesy, sharing, and group relationships are all-important cannot comprehend our brittle, materialistic way of life.

Ask your friend as you teach her about *her* family, *her* customs, *her* religion. Don't give the impression that *her* country is of no interest to you.

Arrange some social evenings, with the husbands involved. Take family picnics together. Invite your friends over for Thanksgiving or Christmas dinner. Go to a football game together. Take her shopping. Show her how to cook the foodstuffs she has never seen before . . . in *your* kitchen. Give her a chance to understand our culture.

Do you know what "culture shock" is all about? It's what happens when one's culture suddenly is invaded with another culture . . . *and you become the battleground.* It's no laughing matter. People react in different ways during this period of time. Some withdraw from the old culture, some from the new. Others become depressed, and others work feverishly. When your friend faces it, there's nothing more meaningful than someone *like you* who has enough love and concern to "hang in" with her.

The reward for HOPE ministries is never greater than when

you go to your mailbox and find a letter from overseas. A former student writes to tell you about her children, her activities, and her continued reading of her Bible. Then comes the punch line: "Please pray for me. I begin to understand what you say to me about Jesus. I miss you! Love, Satsuko."

---

[1] Secure catalog from Regents Publishing Co., Inc., 2 Park Ave., New York, N.Y. 10016. This firm specialized in English As Foreign Language publications. They have everything you will ever need!

7

Women's TOUCH Bible Groups

"What do most women in fast-paced, suburban America have in common?" a veteran of TOUCH Bible groups was asked. *"Loneliness!"* she replied. "Though they may have a loving husband, healthy children, and a beautiful home, their biggest hurt comes from loneliness. It seems that the more successful their husbands are and the bigger their house, the more they feel it."

What many women need, in a unique way, is a friend who understands. (Men have a similar need, of course, but it is harder for them to admit it.) When women recognize this need, they quickly migrate to groups where sensitive friendships can be found. This is why TOUCH Bible groups are among the easiest target groups to establish . . . and why some of them have been meeting regularly for over four years.

Should you feel called to begin Bible groups in your area, your problem will definitely *not* be one of finding interested women! Some will be divorced, others widows. Still others will be married to men who are alcoholics and will be searching for the strength to deal with the problem. Others are trapped in a lonely life-style in which the husband works long hours and then plays golf every weekend.

Fred, ladies who initiate these groups will see frequent evidence of the Holy Spirit leading Outsiders to Christ. He TOUCHes personal hurts through Scripture in an astonishing way. Many workers in these groups have told about "watching the Lord move into lives" as the weeks progress.

This is one type of ministry where recognition of one's

spiritual gifts will have a definite bearing on the manner in which the groups are conducted. A woman with a *gift of teaching* may find her Bible groups focusing upon her capacity to instruct in the Scripture's truths by both word and deed.

However, there is another way TOUCH Bible groups can operate. Those who have the *paraclete gift* will be drawn to use the second method. Note carefully the distinction between them:

1. **The Teaching Method.** In this system, a gifted teacher is absolutely necessary. The group comes together to hear a careful exegesis of a passage by the teacher. This may last for 30 minutes. Questions are saved for the close of the exegesis. Then discussion takes place, often centering upon questions prepared in advance by the teacher to get the dialogue time started. The discussion should not be a "back-and-forth" between teacher and group members, but an open round-table discussion of the life-principles to be drawn from the Scripture passage.

2. **The Paraclete Method.** In this system, there is absolutely *no teaching.* A book like Mark is selected for the study, and "ground rules" are agreed upon by the group. These may include: No "pet" doctrines will be pushed, no theological rabbits will be chased. Leadership of the group is rotated *each week.* The pattern: a full paragraph of Scripture is read, and the leader-for-a-day asks three questions:

(1) What did Mark say? (2) Why did Mark say this? [*That is, with all the things about Jesus Mark could have brought up, why did he choose this detail for us?*] (3) What difference does understanding this section mean to me personally?

The TOUCH ministers remain in the background, normal participants in the discussions. Of utmost importance is the recognition of the *integrity* of each person in the group. Each person is free to state what he believes—or does not believe. The only "ground rule" here is that Mark must *also* be given the right to say what he said . . . and not be rejected for it! Questions which are not answerable by the members of the group may be left "hanging." A copy or two of a good Bible handbook may be loaned to members who want to do some digging on their own.

The TOUCH ministers use the group meetings to discern the personal needs and problems of each Outsider. The attitudes and beliefs of the women will be clearly revealed in this setting. Then, in private more than in the group, the TOUCH workers share their faith, challenging the women to find their own relationship to Jesus Christ.

Much fruit has resulted from the use of *both* methods. The Paraclete Method is initially difficult for Christians who have never before been in Bible groups which are not led by an "authority figure" . . . but this method is often far more fruitful. *Try it!*

A great way to begin a TOUCH Bible Group is for the team to conduct an initial neighborhood kaffee klatsch. Invite neighbors to come with a flower (real or artificial) and their favorite cup. Arrange these flowers in a dish, and draw a name to award the dish of flowers to one of the ladies. You might say at that time, "You know, the Lord does this with people . . . He puts *us* together in arrangements, and makes us a group to grow in him!" As coffee and refreshments are served, the Quaker Questions can be used to get the women acquainted with each other. (If more than eight are present, divide by eights into circles for this activity.)

At the conclusion of the klatsch, a piece of paper can be placed on a table near the door. Ladies are invited to sign it if they would like to meet on a regular basis for a Bible group.

Do not be surprised if only a few (or even no one) accepts the initial invitation. They may be trying to "size you up." This may be a new part of you they have never seen before. Give them some time, and let the Holy Spirit direct you in your follow-up with the group. Drop a note to all, letting them know that the group *has* been launched and that they are welcome to attend at any time. Even if the only two who attend are the TOUCH team, conduct the group meeting! You may want to conduct additional klatsches in the neighborhood until you have eight in the group.

During the first studies together, begin with basics. For some of the ladies this may be their first Bible study since Sunday School days as a child; *for others, the first in their lives!*

The book of Mark is excellent for the first sessions. It is a little easier to understand than the other Gospels (no genealogy lists, for one thing). Chapter 1, verse 1 introduces the "gospel" of Jesus Christ. This is a perfect spot to ask what the word "gospel" means . . . and insert a clear explanation of the "good news" in detail.

Use no "lesson plan" or literature of a denominational nature. There is nothing to limit exactly what you will cover, or how far you will go on a particular day. Some TOUCH groups have not even completed one chapter in ten weeks! What *is* important, however, is to keep everyone talking about the subject introduced by the Scripture, with individual reactions to it. Too much digression takes away from the value of the group. Remember . . . each member must feel free to express exactly "where they are at" in their personal pilgrimage toward Christ. *Don't crowd Outsiders.*

If one of them asks you a question you cannot answer, don't panic! Above all, don't try to fake answers; explain that you do not know the answer, but you will do your best to get one. Then consult your pastor or another whose knowledge of the Word you can rely upon. Give the answer at the next meeting. Don't let it "hang!"

Use a common translation. We have encouraged common use of *The New English Bible.* This makes it possible to suggest the group turn to a specific *page,* as well as book, chapter, and verse. This will avoid the embarrassment some may feel who do not know how to find their way in the Scripture.

Also be careful about embarrassing women by asking them questions they will not be able to answer. Do not presuppose the same background of knowledge concerning the Bible *you* have. Limit questions to those which do not require background knowledge; questions dealing with personal reactions to verses are far safer.

Allow a full hour and a half for each meeting. Serve refreshments at the beginning, not the end. From 9:30 to 11:00 A.M. is a good time; other groups meet from 10:30 to Noon, then share a salad luncheon. As the study nears the closing time, ask for prayer requests. Encourage each lady to write down these requests and take them away to pray about during the week. *By all means, use conversational prayer as the method of praying together.* Stress the fact that some who are in the group may *want* to pray silently, and that this is perfectly acceptable.

Let each lady know individually you are available at any time they have something to share. Chances are many that you will be called. Occasionally, call each woman and ask her how she is getting along. Show a constant concern.

To be effective, the group should be limited to eight. You may wish to work from a "base" of twelve, for often several women will have sick children, etc., and have to miss a meeting. If the group grows larger, divide it into two and select another day or plan for the second group to meet. Be alert for potential leadership within your initial group. Often one or two of them will reach the stage where they can be encouraged to begin a new group in another neighborhood.

The stories of lives which have been changed through these ministries would fill a book! Mothers who had dropped out of church years before have been returned to their congregations. Skeptics who have traveled through endless cults and Eastern religions have finally found the end of their search.

There are the occasional conversions that are unforgettable . . . like the woman who heard the discussion about "Good News" during the first minutes in the study of Mark 1:1, and began to ask question after question. Within the first hour of the first meeting, she confessed her faith in Christ before the entire group. After searching for years through numerous philosophies and cults, she had met the Christ of her search in minutes!

Sometimes the results of the groups are not that dramatic but just as far reaching . . . as illustrated by the woman who finally asked the group what to do about her homelife. Her husband insisted that she attend X-rated movies with him, and he kept a stack of pornographic magazines beside his chair in their living room. She was ready to give up on him. She took the counsel of the other women not to antagonize him. Instead, she placed some Christian literature next to his chair—carefully chosen on the basis of his intellect. The group began to pray together for him. In the weeks that followed, a fine pastor intercepted his life, and he decided to take his wife to church. He was subsequently brought to personal faith in Christ and now lives a changed life.

More and more women are seeking for the God their parents may have ignored. Finding they have nothing within themselves to fall back on when they face the stresses of adult problems, they are finally open to the message of Christ. Feeling too "old" to become a learner in Sunday School, they hesitate to begin to frequent long-ignored churches. Your TOUCH Bible group may prove to be the first step to bringing her entire family to know Christ as Lord!

8

TOUCH "Rap" Sessions

"Kids today are no different than when I was a kid. They just think they are."
Right?
Wrong!
Nothing could be further from the truth. Aside from the biological changes that occur in a young man and woman's body at puberty, there are few similiarities between growing up today and growing up a generation or more ago.

Fred, the world has become complex. Old values have been changed. Today's teenagers have unstable authority figures in their lives, and uncertain relationships in their families. Add to the soaring divorce rate the problems of alcoholism, mental illness, and social sicknesses. They exist at greater levels than ever before: it's no wonder teenagers are confused!

Many of them are tired of "hearing" from adults. They can see that adult values have created the problems they must now face. *They want answers*—and the TOUCH "Rap" format can help give some to them.

"Rap" is simply a slang word for group dialogue. Teenagers get together and talk about problems and frustrations, about what is and is not meaningful in their lives.

Apartment complexes have become miniature metropolises within big cities. Where there are large concentrations of people, the atmosphere does not lend itself to knowing people intimately, even if they are only the thickness of a piece of wallboard away. Rap sessions in apartment complexes provide a good way to help tear down some of the walls between youngsters and their parents, each other, and authority figures in their lives. Above all, these sessions are an enormously effective way to TOUCH adolescents for Christ.

To begin a Rap session in an apartment complex, begin with a visit to the manager. Ask for help. Many managers experience their biggest headaches with the teens in their development. Vandalism is the result of youngsters who are torn up within themselves. Most managers are ready to try *anything* that appears to have even a slim chance of success.

Large complexes have pools with a clubhouse adjacent to it. Ask for its use. It is an excellent setting for Rap sessions, and it usually is only booked on weekends. Quite frequently the manager must also act as a "social director," and he himself will have the reservation book for this facility. In other cases, there will be a poorly-paid employee who fills this role—perhaps doing little more than baby-sitting and guarding the property. In either case, your careful description of what you will be doing—*without charge*—will be gratefully appreciated. Of course, if you offered to do this same thing under the sponsorship of a church, you would be quickly refused!

Get the addresses of the teenagers in the complex from this manager. If this is not possible, hang around the pool when the teens are there, and spread the word by mouth. In most cases, however, we have had no problem in getting a list of the high schoolers and in writing them a letter of invitation to the first Rap. This letter should be humorous and mysterious, utilizing phrases like, "What is RAP?" "Who NEEDS it?" "Is it a drag?" "What's *this* guy's bag?"

Your initial Rap is critical to your survival. Selling the manager was the *easy* part; now comes the tough part . . . selling the kids!

Use a weeknight for the meeting. Kids have things to do on weekends and will not attend something like this. During the week, it gives them a legitimate reason for getting out of the apartment. Hold it at an early evening hour, so parents won't complain about the late sessions on a school night. Of course, you'll want to be sure you don't compete with the "Club Nights" many urban high schools hold on Monday or Tuesday evenings. In Houston, we found Monday evenings our best time, but it took several tries before we discovered this.

The teenagers will decide very quickly whether the leader is sincere, flexible or rigid, aware of their needs or "out of it." If those who want to work in this ministry do not feel they are truly aware of how teens feel, they should delay the beginnings of Raps and prepare themselves. How? Talk to kids! Where? Wherever you see them . . . sitting on the trunks of cars outside an ice cream shop, in pool halls, *in record shops.* You can learn a lot by just spending an evening sitting in the corner of the restaurant or whatever they frequent regularly . . . and listening! A conversation with the counselor at your local high school will also be of significance. What things should you pick up? Among other things, *their local slang.* What do they call marijuana? A pregnant girl? Hard drugs? Do you know what a "Jock" is? A "Cowboy"? Teen slang moves in and out of fashion faster than hit records, and *nothing* is more idiotic than someone who is using last year's vocabulary.

Such times of listening may give you a list of 15 topics to use in Raps. Here are a few to get you started:

(1) What do you think about the dress code? Practically all high schools have one; practically none of the students like it! You can easily spend an hour "rapping" about this subject and wonder where it went. (You also may decide the kids have a side worth thinking about.) Of course, this is not the primary reason you are getting together with these youngsters. From the discussion about dress codes you need to move into a spiritual emphasis . . . like a discussion of the code for living called the Ten Commandments God has

given to us. How do they feel about *that?*

(2) *What do you think about authority? What is its place in life?* How do they feel about parental authority? School officials? Police? What would life be like without any authority systems? Should students have the power to override authorities, and make their own rules? Who decides these matters? Does the majority feeling about something mean that the system should "bend" to their wishes? Who makes rules for living?

Do you begin to get the picture? Fix upon the things that confuse or frustrate young people . . . *deep topics* that deal with basic issues. The topic of abortion may be meaningful or trite, depending on whether every teenager has or has not already decided there is nothing wrong with it.

The matter of cheating on tests is a powerful topic to discuss! So is a frank discussion of sexual standards. Encourage the group to suggest topics they would like to discuss. Often this works best when they are not asked to verbalize this before the entire group. When you find the group rapping about a topic which is "off the subject," you probably have a topic for an entire evening . . . *soon!*

After a few weeks, have a "Special." This can take the form of a Christian disc jockey or sports figure. Perhaps a local group of college athletes has a well-known player who would be glad to come over. The "celebrity" should not be introduced as a *speaker* (ugh!), but one who is coming to *rap.* Let the personal testimony form a natural part of the conversation. Avoid the very appearance of an "I'm up here—you're down there" structure. Total availability is the key to success . . . along with total *vulnerability.*

Oh, yes: another important point . . . keep adults away! Though you may wish to have a few beside the leader, they should keep a low profile in the physical setting, and stay out of the rapping, no matter how much they wish to express their opinions. Young couples will function in many situations better than parent-aged adults, but there are some beautiful exceptions to this rule.

The success of rap sessions hinges on getting the kids to express themselves and letting them have their say. In most situations in their lives—at home, at school, at church (if they go!)—they are talked *to* and taught *by* adults. No one gives them much opportunity to say anything. If they do talk up, what they say is frequently passed over. You may be surprised at how just letting them talk among themselves will eventually bring them to sensible conclusions. Therefore, do not feel that you must *necessarily* conclude each session with some sage advice or devotional.

Your purpose primarily is to listen to them share and to stimulate their conversation. In the midst of this, you will quickly discover the fears and needs of each one. With this awareness, you are in a position to minister to them on an individual basis. It will make it possible for you to move into spiritual matters in such a way that they will not feel they are being "preached to."

Psychiatrists might call Rap sessions group therapy. If the kids like it, you will no longer need to worry about *what* it is called. It will begin to grow—and grow—and grow. Word of mouth is the best possible publicity for Raps.

Follow-up is important, particularly with those who have expressed an interest in knowing more about spiritual things. Eventually church staff members can be of help in providing suggestions about what to do in leading new converts into the life of the local church.

As the group grows, there will be two "levels" of development. Those who come in for the first time will not be ready for the same level of spiritual discussion as some of those who have been coming for some time. A good way to solve this problem is to "siphon off" those who are ready to get down to spiritual basics and conduct a Bible study for them at a different time. It may possibly cause some of them to

drop out of the Rap because of time pressures, but that is
nothing to be alarmed about.

At the Bible studies, all subtleties can be dropped. Get
right down to conversations about the meaning of being a
Christian.

The technique for beginning Rap sessions in a community
of single family homes is similar to that described for apartments. The major difference focuses upon the relationships
you will build to parents. They are going to be more concerned about where their children are going at night—in the
complex, they are still "in range" if needed for something
at home. When you use a den in a home for your Rap, ask
the parents to either "take a night out" or keep out of sight.

It's extremely important to prepare the members of the
church and your youth group for the influx of converts from
Rap sessions. There must be some delicate dynamics in your
church group when they arrive! Some churches have found
a real "generation gap" between the turned-on new converts
and the youngsters who have been attending church all their
lives. While the Rap converts sit on the front row taking
notes on the sermon, the "church kids" may be sitting on
the back row writing notes and snickering. If they freeze
out the converts, the scars of this rejection may remain for
years and years.

Our suggestion is that you involve your own church
members who are in high schools in both the Rap sessions
and the Bible studies. As with adults, however, they should
keep a "low profile." Their preachy-type witnessing in the
Rap may turn off those who are not yet ready to accept the
Christian faith. However, their participation will assist in
avoiding the "white mice versus the black mice" syndrome
which might well occur otherwise.

Fred, once you have a few teams of Christians working
in Rap sessions, your prayer meetings on Wednesday evenings will be *prayer* meetings. Those young 'uns will become

a lead weight on the hearts of those who become related to them. Oh, . . . let me add that those who enter *this* ministry will soon find their spare time crowded with teens dropping by to talk about every imaginable problem. *Raps are a way of life* for People Who Care!

9

TOUCH Clubs:
Reaching Elementary Children

Several years ago, pioneer churches in the Minnesota-Wisconsin area were reporting a pitiful dozen baptisms for a total year of work. Suddenly, everything exploded! In one year these same congregations reported an astonishing number of conversions from all ages in their annual minutes. I was fascinated to learn the "secret" behind their sudden harvest: they had established back-yard Bible clubs for grade school children. *The Insiders had finally found a way to relate to Outsiders!*

While certainly not true of all cultures, in the American situation many families can be "entered" through doing something meaningful for a child in the household. Weekday TOUCH Clubs are a perfect way to relate to youngsters. Follow-up affords opportunity to relate to the parents.

TOUCH Clubs can take on many forms. Several years ago I experimented with a boy's club which sponsored the building of model airplanes. I purchased a dozen gas-powered model engines and as many kits. Boys from a local trailer camp were unable to pay any money for these items, so I arranged a "work payment" for them . . . mowing lawns, trimming hedges, and other things. They were given a sense of self-respect from this activity, for they gradually "bought" the models while they were building them. The final thirty minutes of each club meeting focused upon a study of the life of Jesus. Many of these lads eventually became the first ones in their family to ever follow Christ.

TOUCH Clubs for elementary school children can focus around many activities: baton twirling, cooking, sewing, baseball or another sport. Of course, one of the most logical focal points would be around the *study of the Bible.*

For many months, a dozen or more women met in Houston every Monday morning to prepare for TOUCH Clubs in apartment complexes. So great was the demand for these club meetings that our congregation finally asked the women of a nearby Lutheran church to assist. *The requests came from the managers of apartment complexes!* One of them even tried to lure us with a check for $50 to buy Bibles and supplies for the kids. They knew that a large percentage of these youngsters were unsupervised during the late afternoon because both parents worked. *There was a marked reduction in vandalism in their complexes when the kids had a TOUCH Club.*

After a few months of club activity, I began to look out over our congregation and see many of these boys and girls attending worship services with their parents. Then we began to reap the harvest. I particularly think of a girl, then her brother, and finally their dad, who came into our fellowship because of a TOUCH Club held next door to their house.

A college student in our congregation worked in a ghetto area of the city each summer reaching children from the most sordid circumstances with "Five-Day Clubs" held in back yards. These were exactly what the name implies: *clubs which lasted for five days,* meeting each morning or afternoon for one and a half hours.

To assure continuity with other TOUCH ministries in the same area, ladies who participated often wore nylon jackets bearing the TOUCH emblem, or blue smocks with the symbol embroidered on them. TOUCH pins were also worn by some of the workers. [1]

Here are suggestions from one who coordinated these clubs for a period of time in apartment houses:

1. **Bathe the work in prayer.** Especially pray for the leadership of the Holy Spirit in selecting the apartment complexes and neighborhoods where these clubs should begin. Pray for

wisdom in selecting the proper *types* of clubs to be started. Pray much about the assignments of workers to areas.

2. **Arrange time and place.** Contact the managers of the complexes where you wish to start clubs. Ask permission to use the Club Room or Social Room. *Personal contacts* are necessary . . . don't attempt this by telephone calls. Explain what the TOUCH Clubs are, and point out they will be something *constructive* for children to be doing during hours when they usually are free to destroy property. Emphasize no charge will be made for this service and that it is not an attempt to proselyte people who attend a church or synagogue. After a weekly day and time have been agreed upon, explain that with his permission you will visit each apartment to invite children to attend.

3. **Extend invitations.** Some complexes have a monthly newsletter for all residents. We found it possible to introduce the clubs to tenants in this manner. When this is not possible, hand out invitations door-to-door at least one day before the first club meeting. One of the merits of passing out invitations door-to-door is that you may uncover Christians who will be interested in helping with refreshments and keeping records for the club.

Parents will be unhappy if you try to "ignore" them and work with their children unannounced. It only takes one irate parent putting pressure on the management for you to lose your foothold! (The same thing holds true in a neighborhood setting.)

4. **Introduce the workers.** Give each new worker a *personal* introduction to apartment managers. Take nothing for granted. A strong "public relations" program will create much goodwill. Give each worker all names and telephone numbers of children interested in attending the club. And remember . . . try to use the services of as many people who live in the apartment complex as possible.

5. **Hold occasional parties or picnics.** About once each

quarter invite all the children from all the clubs to meet in a park or recreational area for a fun-time. Have special events and special entertainment. Use these occasions for testimonies from children who have received Christ. Involve parents in the recreation, food, etc., for these parties.

6. **Seek to deepen relationships with the family units.** Do not ignore the opportunity to get acquainted with the parents and other siblings of the child represented in your club. Before you know it, you will see a need for other TOUCH ministries within the complex: divorcees, older brother and sisters on drugs, alcoholic parent, and others will become evident. Mother's Bible study groups may well be a necessary addition to the TOUCH Clubs within a few weeks.

It would be wiser to restrict the membership to each club so you have time for adequate follow-up than to *pack kids in* and treat them as "digits." You must discipline yourself to *reach family units,* not just meet with a group of kids once a week. Otherwise, you will forfeit your evangelistic opportunity! Two TOUCH workers should limit the club meeting to ten family units . . . five for each worker. That's a case load heavy enough to break your heart.

7. **Do not neglect the nurture of young converts.** Soon after you begin, you will find the first fruits of your sowing and cultivating ready for harvest. By involvement with the parents, you will know if it is possible for the child to openly confess the new commitment to Christ before the parents. If it *is* possible, go with the child when this is done. Discuss frankly your desire to spend additional time with the youngster teaching basics of Christian growth . . . and ask permission to do so with a parent present. Perhaps a regular time in the evening can be set up for you to do this in the family's apartment. The result of this has often been the conversion of the parent. You will discover they do not "listen" very long; soon they are in the middle of the study, and asking most of the questions!

8. Introduce the children from Christian homes to those in the clubs. A good time to do this is during the occasional parties or picnics. Always bear in mind that there is a "culture shock" to be faced when an Outsider comes *inside;* the more familiar faces recognized on that first visit to the church services, the less the shock will be felt.

---

[1] See Appendix.

10

Tracts That TOUCH

Fred, I've got a long distance call . . . probably from some friend who has read one of the earlier books about TOUCH who is calling to "report in" about the exciting things going on since the Insiders got outside! While I'm taking the call, Cal, I'd like you to tell him about the plastic racks we have made for distribution all over our community. I'll be back in a few minutes.

As a newsman, Fred, you'd expect me to tell you that I believe the pen is mightier than the sword; it is also mightier than the spoken word.

Sermons and one-to-one witnessing, as powerful as they may be, are sometimes less potent than the written word. We have found that a printed piece can so disturb a stranger that we have never met that they have called us from a hospital waiting room at 3 o'clock in the morning!

God has caused his word to be recorded so we might study it, memorize it, and meditate on it. It can also evangelize! While it is true that the gospel and not the printed page leads a person to Christ, the gospel on a printed page can sometimes be a means of TOUCHing people. One of the most effective ways the written word can be used (and perhaps the least understood) is the *tract.*

Fred, I used to think tracts were written and distributed by religious fanatics. You know the type: a guy who wears white shirts, thin ties, never smiles, and generally looks like he doesn't enjoy being alive. He even looks like he doesn't enjoy passing out tracts!

One day someone passed a tract to me as I was working

on a story. It was well-written, thought-provoking, and made its point without insulting my intelligence. It didn't conjure any of those stereotypes that turn people off to the Christian life. I saw the tract from a new perspective.

An important thing to remember about tracts is that they are designed for different situations, and for different people. Each tract should be evaluated before it is used. It should be relevant to a particular person and situation. Think of them as fitting into two classifications: *witnessing* tracts, and *winning* tracts.

A *witnessing* tract is designed to cut right through a person's facade and plunge deeply into his heart. It is also designed to be a part of a more meaningful and greater relationship between the Christian and the Outsider. *The Way* magazine, mentioned in the earlier discussion we had about the TOUCH Night People ministry, is an example of this. Such a tract does not detail the plan of salvation. It limits its message to a single, disturbing thought. It "rattles the cage" of the Outsider.

On the other hand, a *winning* tract carefully details the plan of salvation for the reader. It is designed to be used with someone who is sincerely interested in what the Christian life means, or to be given to someone who will never be in touch with you again. When you select such a tract, be sure all Scriptures are fully written out . . . and that it is free from religious jargon. Several pocket-size booklets are available today which perfectly meet this requirement. The length of the winning tract may exceed that of a witnessing tract, since its primary purpose is *teaching*, rather than *motivating*.

Fred, let me tell you a true story that you may have heard before: A man stood at a bus stop in a large city. He had recently been discharged from the Army where he had served as a medic. He was despondent, unsure of himself, and bewildered about what he would do in civilian life. Suddenly a car approached, slowed to a near stop, and an arm shot out of the window and offered a piece of paper to the young man. He took it, and the car continued down the street. The message on that paper told about how Jesus Christ meets *any* need in life. A telephone number was listed, where one could call and find a helping person. That young man made a telephone call, and a relationship was established which led to his conversion. He had been given a *winning* tract.

If you're still even the least skeptical, let me tell you about the impact of a tract upon the Lisus of western China. J. O. Frasier, missionary to the Northern Lisu tribes, had a great prayer burden for those in the South Lisu district. He had never been able to preach to those tribal groups, but on one occasion met one in a marketplace. He gave him a tract, and never saw him again. However, that tract won a man, who won a group, who preached Christ to one South Lisu tribe after another. The entire district of South Lisus were in the midst of a mighty revival *before the first missionary ever arrived to work among them!*

Tracts have impact, and we ought to be using them by the tens of thousands. However, each one should be evaluated before it is distributed. The following points are helpful to remember:

1. Does it answer a question someone is *really* asking?
2. Is it brief?
3. Does it speak positively, without knocking another faith?
4. Is the type large, the format colorful and well done?
5. Is it a *winning* or a *witnessing* tract? (If not, for the purposes of TOUCH, it's a *worthless* tract!)
6. Does it relate to what people are feeling, on the basis of their knowledge?
7. Does it use religious jargon or cliches Outsiders won't understand?
8. Does it sound "preachy," or does it simply share the

good news?

A tract is not designed to take the place of a verbal, more personal witness. It is a supplement, not a substitute, for this life-to-life relationship. Sometimes, because of circumstances, it must serve as a substitute for a personal witness in the "seed sowing" process in evangelism. Never use it if a personal relationship would be more effective.

On occasion, it can be given with a suggestion that you would like to have the receiver share with you his reaction to its content. It can often be used in this fashion to open relational evangelistic dialogue.

Our TOUCH tract ministry was initiated by a husband and wife who felt a real burden to share Christ in our community through the written word. They selected the word "SMILE" for the ministry: Silent Ministry In Love Extended. As they have explained, "Often only the Lord knows the full impact of our ministry. We have always been interested in reaching others for him, and often shared Christ with Outsiders. We felt SMILE would be a way to share with many who might refuse our verbal testimony."

And share they have . . . in the most out-of-the-way places! The church purchased plexiglass strips, cut to size for racks which were assembled in their garage. A lovely aluminized sticker with the TOUCH word and symbol offered the contents of the attractive rack free and included a telephone number for those who wanted further assistance.

In order that the racks would be accepted by diverse groups, the largest item in the rack—eleven inches high—was a church directory, listing *all* churches and synagogues within the community. The next tallest items were witnessing tracts, including *The Way* magazine. This changed monthly, giving a reason for people to return to the rack more than one time. The smallest items were in the front of the rack and were winning tracts.

These racks were placed all over the community! Campers

who passed through a local park found them in the shower rooms. In many self-service laundries of apartment houses, people who waited for clothes to be tumbled dry in machines found interesting reading matter available. Still others found a rack attached to a wall in the area where they picked up their mail.

That is only a start of where they have been placed: hospitals, rest rooms, offices of doctors and dentists, executive's reception rooms, restaurants, dry cleaners, hotels, motel rooms, local businesses, barber shops, beauty salons, liquor store (!), porches, grocery stores. There are many other possibilities.

Once placed, the plastic racks had to be serviced on a continual basis. A few met with vandals. Often a certain tract or booklet would be taken, while others were left. These were used more intensively. *Fred, it's a job to make the rounds of all the places racks are mounted.* . . . More than that, it's a *ministry!* As that ministry grew, the Lord called another TOUCH minister. This godly woman was challenged by the literature itself, brought home by her son from a meeting. She began to see the possible impact upon the community and called the couple to volunteer her services. She was a direct answer to their prayers. They were exhausted by the growing "routes" which had been established.

At the start, they were not using what quickly became the most popular item in the racks: *Christian comic books.* When they discovered that several publishers had released them, they began to order them by the hundreds. In Texas, one of the most popular was the comic book story of the life of Cowboy football coach Tom Landry. A close second was "Archie's Clean Slate." Real-life stories included "God's Smuggler," "The Hiding Place," and others. They became so popular that they were "traded" between children in one apartment complex.

The value of this type of ministry is in the "climatizing"

of a community for Christ. In a secular society every type of reading matter is pushed by every type of store. Pornography is readily accessible. It leaves a feeling with people that God is not around! When the quiet placement of racks takes place, and when they are frequently checked and refilled, the community is made aware of the presence of Christian lives in the midst. It creates a *climate* of awareness. That's important to all the other TOUCH ministries that are taking place at the same time.

Can you imagine what impact we would have in the nation if *each congregation* maintained 50 racks each? Why, the members of churches alone control enough places to mount that many racks. The climate of a nation can be changed by such a strategy. Communists, I'm told, print THREE PIECES OF LITERATURE ANNUALLY for each person on earth. When do *we* start TOUCHing through tracts?

11

TOUCHing Men
Through Prayer Breakfasts

This time, Fred, I'm taking notes along with you! This is Cal's TOUCH ministry, and he's as fired up about it as a kid with bees inside his shirt. I hope you catch the flame! Okay, Cal . . . wax eloquent . . .

Fred, the purpose of a prayer breakfast is to get business, professional, and political men to meet "in the spirit of Christ" for the purpose of inserting Christ into the worlds of business and professions. City governments have been TOUCHed by them. They create a maturing relationship between men and Jesus Christ.

Most men go to lunch. For many, the business lunch has become a part of the business day. It is predictable. However, the idea of getting together with men of similar backgrounds and education at 7:00 or 7:30 in the morning *to discuss something besides business* is unusual! For many men, curiosity alone will get them to their first prayer breakfast. Something else will bring them back the next time!

The prayer breakfast idea actually began in the late 1930's in Seattle, Washington. The mayor of Seattle was deeply concerned about the direction in which his city was heading. Both morally and economically Seattle was in trouble. The mayor confided in a Christian friend, unloading his great burden. His friend said, "Let's get the business, professional, and political leaders together for a breakfast and ask God *to heal this city.*" The mayor agreed. Claiming the promise given in 2 Chronicles 7:14, they met together at a Seattle restaurant. They prayed—confessing their sins; they turned from their old ways, and they humbled themselves. In the weeks that followed, God healed Seattle of both its moral and economic sicknesses.

Today, prayer breakfasts are being held all over the world. In the nation's Capitol, the House and Senate hold weekly prayer breakfasts, well attended by many members. Once a year, these House and Senate prayer groups invite the President of the United States to attend a national prayer breakfast. Leaders from all over the country and the world gather that morning to ask God's guidance in their lives and in their work.

The benefits which come from the fellowship of prayer breakfasts are many. "Fellowship" is a basically *Christian* word, referring to something infinitely more nourishing and satisfying than either the casual or formal relationships in our American society.

At most modern social functions, men come together like marbles. They just "bump against" each other then ricochet around the room. Conversation is kept at a shallow, extraneous level. The atmosphere is usually noisy, confused, hollow. Nobody gets intimate enough to share things with deep meaning. Bored V.I.P.'s tolerate the advances of namedroppers and opportunists. *What* one knows is immaterial; *who* one knows is desperately important. The cocktail party is a microcosm of modern man's social bankruptcy.

Fellowship is at the other end of the spectrum! In a prayer breakfast men come together like grapes—crushed, with skins of ego broken. The rich, fragrant, exhilarating juices of life mingle in the wine of sharing. It's a time for understanding and caring.

Fellowship is the fusion of personalities through the person and presence of Jesus. It only occurs when men gather in Jesus' name. It is horizontal—man with man, and vertical—man with God.

Civic clubs, good as they are, do not provide the kind

of fellowship Jesus wanted men to know. Fellowship is the type of relationship that will endure long after clubs and other organization-oriented relationships have disappeared.

At the heart of fellowship is a spiritual bond, with Christ at the center. It remains after you quit the clubs, when you are fired from your job, or go bankrupt. It can't be taken away because its foundation rests on One who is always reliable, who will love you no matter how many times you let him down.

Before I knew anything about a personal God, I used to think that the greatest relationships between men were in the sports world. When someone would score a touchdown, sink the winning basket, or a fight would break out on the field, men got involved in what was going on. They would hug each other, or benches would empty to cheer a fellow player in trouble. Teams traveled together and shared rooms. A player would encourage his teammate by giving him a pat on the rump. This seemed to me to be the *ultimate* in friendship!

But Fred, athletes graduate from college, get traded in the professional ranks, or just retire. *Then* what kind of relationship do they have? Is it eternal? Of course not.

I began to realize that the essence of fellowship is not based on what *I* have done, or the clubs and groups in which I am involved. A truly lasting relationship begins with—and endures in—Jesus Christ.

Jesus said, "Where two or three are gathered together in my name, there am I in the midst of them." In 1 John 1:3 we read, "That which we have seen and heard declare we unto you, that ye also may have fellowship with us; and truly our fellowship is with the Father, and with his Son Jesus Christ."

This is fellowship at the prayer breakfast level: meeting together in the Spirit of Christ, for a common, perhaps unspoken, reason.

But how do you begin a prayer breakfast if you're not in Washington and if you don't know any important political or business leaders? Can you expect just *anyone* to call people on the telephone and ask them to breakfast? Precisely! Exactly!

Fred, Cal has proved how true this is. He has even invited an astronaut to his house for a 7:00 A.M. breakfast. He came—30 miles! This man talking to you practices what he preaches . . . I've watched him in action.

First of all, if you are a Spirit-filled Christian, people at your office already know that you're "different." Asking them to breakfast won't seem odd: they *already* think you're odd. They'll probably come to find out why!

There is no structured format. A typical breakfast might begin with prayer, a Scripture reading, and then a lay speaker who has been invited for that morning. He might speak for about twenty minutes. His topic can center upon anything he chooses. Usually, Bible study is not the focal point. There are many other opportunities for Bible study. The central emphasis in this ministry is upon relationships. Many of the men you invite will not know Christ as Lord and Savior. A Bible study might appear to them to be more of what they have already seen and rejected. It might also appear that you are trying to get them to join your church!

Therefore, a speaker might share from his own experiences as a Christian involved in his world. His remarks may be related to what he does as a lawyer, doctor, or business executive. He will share how Christ has dealt with him. He will present Christ in a nonstereotyped way. He will simply be a man with whom other men can identify.

A prayer breakfast is an expression of what the Christian life is all about. The Christian life is relational: man with God, man to man. The time spent together helps men to know how to grow in their relationships to God and to others. Frankness and transparency will mark the level of conver-

sations which will take place with the speaker and each other
following the formal presentation.

So, Fred, if you feel a burden for *your* office or your
community, contact some other Christian men and see if they
feel the same way. If the group is small, start in someone's
home . . . if the cooking is not too much of a chore for
the wife. My own wife, for example, looks on her cooking
as an integral part of *our* prayer breakfast ministry.

A restaurant is an alternative possibility for the location
of the breakfast. Most restaurants will cordon off an area
for groups, particularly when they know they can count on
the business on a regular basis. Of course, private rooms
are *great*—if they don't cost extra.

Contact each new man by letter or telephone explaining
that a group of men are getting together for a prayer breakfast.
It might be a good idea to mention the backgrounds of the
other men, so he won't think it's just another "religious"
function. Mention the *purpose* of the breakfast: fellowship,
praying about common needs and goals, asking for God's
guidance in business matters, healing for a dying city. You
might also mention the name of the speaker as an added
incentive. Give the person the date, time, and location of
the breakfast. A follow-up telephone call the day before the
breakfast will freshen his memory.

Coffee should be ready to drink when the men arrive.
After each man has "doctored" his cup, the leader should
begin with prayer or a verse of Scripture. The speaker is
then introduced. If there is time when he finishes, a brief
question-and-answer time should follow. Conversation con-
tinues during breakfast.

There are many variations to the way you can arrange
the program. For example, the men could eat first, then have
prayer and listen to the speaker. Be flexible!

After the first breakfast meeting, always telephone the
regular attenders the day before the next breakfast. Some

groups meet weekly, others every two weeks, or even once a month. Keep working on new possibilities for the program: one by-product of men speaking to the breakfast is their frequent decision to return as a member of the group!

Begin small to permit a spirit of intimacy to develop in the group. Even if all the men are from the same office, this will be a new setting for them. They will need to learn how to relate in a new kind of way to each other. Give them time to establish new patterns. Another thing, Fred . . . if you start the breakfast with men who are all Christians, within two or three weeks you should be including men who are Outsiders. If you limit the breakfast only to believers, it will quickly stagnate! Keep plugging away at the key men in your community. With a varied attendance, the group will stay as fresh as the coffee you serve.

You'll find an Outsider will add a special dimension to the breakfast. He'll be firing questions into the conversations others would not dare to bring up. In the process, everyone will learn. It can get as exciting as a football game . . . believe me!

One man comes to my memory, who had given up church in disgust. It was not meeting any need in his life. After trying a second church with no more satisfaction than before, he became a drop out. Then the invitation—persistent, I must admit—came to him to attend the prayer breakfast. The business colleague who brought him was delighted to notice an immediate positive reaction by his friend. The man was so moved by the relationships of the breakfast that he began to attend on his own without further encouragement. There followed a commitment of a home and family to Jesus Christ. Together they joined the church of the man who pressed his friend to come to the breakfast. He now is continuing to grow in the Lord.

Other Outsiders attend prayer breakfasts sporadically, listening and thinking, listening and thinking. They cannot avoid the fact that men at the breakfast have something they themselves do not have. One by one, they come to accept Christ as Lord. *Prayer breakfasts reach men!*

12

Divorcees Need a Loving TOUCH

Sarah stared through the side window of her rain-swept car. Across the street, a light appeared in the window of the brick house with dark green shutters . . . her bedroom. At least, it had been her bedroom for eleven years, before she and Jim dissolved their marriage. Now it belonged to a couple from Wisconsin, who purchased it during the settlement of the divorce procedures.

She tortured herself by remembering the "little things" that had taken place in that house: Christmases, when the kids would tumble down the stairs with squeals of delight at all the presents under the tree; late-night returns from fishing trips, when little rag-doll children had to be redressed for bed. In the happy days, she and Jim would come back to the kitchen, clean the fish, and tease each other about who caught the largest one.

Then she remembered the telltale signs that Jim was seeing another woman. She remembered the nights—and half-nights—when that bedroom had been a place of worry and dread for her!

Finally, sitting in the car with the motor still running, the tears turned into great, heaving sobs. Tides of emotion swelled up and out—with no one to comfort her. It wasn't over, this marriage of hers! Inside her head and heart, it went right on in spite of the paper signed by the judge. Weeks had dragged by since that moment in the courtroom, but the memories were still alive and well inside her. When would she be free?

She put her car in gear, and drove away. "Divorcee": how she hated the word! For her, it meant a tiny apartment, children left alone until she returned from the first job she had held in a dozen years, and loneliness. "Goodbye, house," she said aloud. "I hope the family who lives in you now turns out better than ours has."

DIVORCED *Gals...*

Fred, Ruthie and I felt a special calling to begin working with divorcees soon after moving to Houston to pastor the People Who Care. For over three years, we met every other Monday night in our living room with women whose lives had been shattered by divorce, gradually training others to minister in this important area through TOUCH Divorcee Care Groups. The "Alumni List" of those who found healing and a new relationship to Christ is now a part of our prayer list. Nothing we have ever done as a husband-wife team has been as rewarding in terms of instant spiritual response as this particular TOUCH ministry.

Let me share with you the details of how we worked with hurting lives. Now, let's see . . . I have scrawled some notes on the back of an envelope . . . ah! Here they are!

First of all, let me suggest you *make personal preparation* before attempting to organize your first group. Include these items:

1. **Read books about divorce.** Your public library or local bookstore has several volumes written to be read by people contemplating divorce, or who are making the post-divorce adjustment.[1] Devour them! I have encouraged every one of our friends who have started to work in this ministry to read—and underline—*Your Inner Child of the Past* by Dr. Hugh Missildine. It will provide insights into the personal traits of those you work with and will help you understand the absent marriage partner who will be discussed in depth.

In addition, collect a number of books about divorce and the theological views taken about it. I have developed my own convictions on the subject after years of struggling with the "traditional" church attitudes. I have better sense than to express them here in the brief time we have to visit together, Fred, but even if we had time to do so I feel this is an area where we need to do some *personal* agonizing, and not ride "piggyback" on the convictions of another. Within the past few months, a number of books on this topic have been released. Your local Christian bookstore manager can tell you what is available. I'm the kind of fellow who would order them *all*, and prayerfully search the Scriptures after reading them. The final test of your conclusions is going to come in the crucible of sharing them with eight divorced women in a living room! Be *sure* of yourself before attempting that!

2. **Sit in a courtroom and observe divorce.** A morning spent in the courtroom of the judge who handles divorce decrees is an unforgettable experience. Every woman you will work with has been there, and you need to know what people go through during such times. I have accompanied a few women in our groups to that room (as a friend) when their divorce was granted. Observe not only the procedures but also the emotions of both parties while waiting, while the action occurs, and what happens in the hallway afterward. Get acquainted with the trauma of the experience.

3. **Discover groups currently working with divorcees, if any.** Some communities have a chapter of Parents Without Partners. Other churches may have couple's clubs, and occasionally (*tragically so!*) a church will have even organized a "Solos" Sunday School class. Much information can be gleaned by talking to the leaders of such groups and even by sitting in on their sessions. You will want to evaluate what other resources you can—and cannot—recommend to those in your groups.

Second, here are some ideas about making contact with divorcees:

1. **Ask your pastor for names.** In many cases, he will be able to provide you with a list large enough to organize your first group. From time to time, he will relate persons to you who come to him for help.

2. **Tell your local welfare department about the group.** Often their workers face women with great needs as a result of divorce. They will be delighted to know you are doing

something to help.

3. **Notify the attorneys in your area.** They will be glad to refer clients to your group. Often they must serve as therapist as well as legal guide to women, for there is no other resource open for this help.

4. **Tell judges in the divorce court about your work.** The judge is often caught in a situation where your group will answer an obvious need in a woman's life at the time of the hearing.

5. **Put notices in apartment complexes and grocery stores.** We have even put them in elevators of office buildings where scores of divorcees work as secretaries. If you have large factories in your area, notices in the women's lounges will be helpful.

In fact, Fred, the problem you will have in a few weeks after beginning this TOUCH ministry will be how to service all those who come for help! For over two years, we had a constant waiting list of women who wanted to join a group. You will face the same situation!

Third, let me share *how we conducted the sessions:*

1. **We met every other Monday night.** I'm not sure this is the best night in all communities, but I'm going to *guess* that it is. There are unique reasons for this, Fred. Women have children to care for on weekends. That keeps them busy, but by Monday night the "blues" come. The feeling seems to be, "another week—again!" We have come to a conclusion by experimenting that Monday nights are *special* for these groups.

2. **We started late.** Divorcees with children must finish supper and give them attention before leaving for group meetings. The time we set for starting was 8:00 P.M., but we usually "small talked" until 8:30. We frequently broke up at 10:00 P.M., and then the girls would linger until 11:00 or after. When inviting special speakers, don't expect to use them before 8:15 or 8:30.

3. **We let the women bring refreshments.** We provided coffee, but they were asked to bring soft drinks and whatever desserts they desired. For the most part, they were "watching figures," and small cookies were sufficient for refreshments. These were all made available at the *beginning* of the sessions.

4. **We met in the same place each week.** In our case, we used our home. We might have used a club house of an apartment building. We never rotated between the houses or apartments of the women for several reasons: children under foot, interruptions by friends, embarrassment by the women because the apartment was so sparsely furnished. For the sake of privacy the room should be soundproof, not too massive, and chairs placed in a circle, in close proximity to each other. (A dining room with a large round table would be perfect for the group meeting!)

5. **We met for 1½ hours.** This amount of time is *absolutely necessary*. One hour is simply too short for adequate group interaction among the women. The last thirty minutes are often dramatic as hearts overflow after an hour of quiet listening to others. (Don't forget ash trays!)

6. **We limited the groups to ten weeks.** This is a short-term TOUCH ministry. Divorcees hesitated to join us when the groups were "open ended." Their commitment was for ten sessions only. If they desired to continue, we encouraged them to become a "helper" in a new group. Some of the women we worked with shared in the ministry for over two years . . . ten weeks at a time.

7. **We closed the groups to new enrolees.** The trust relationship needed in a divorcee group makes it impossible to add new women successfully after the group has been started. Therefore, we would begin the first session with about 11 or 12 women, and "close" it after the first night to newcomers. By the end of the third session, 4 or 5 would drop out for numerous reasons, leaving 7 or 8 to grow together. There will be a temptation to add new ones as the first group gets

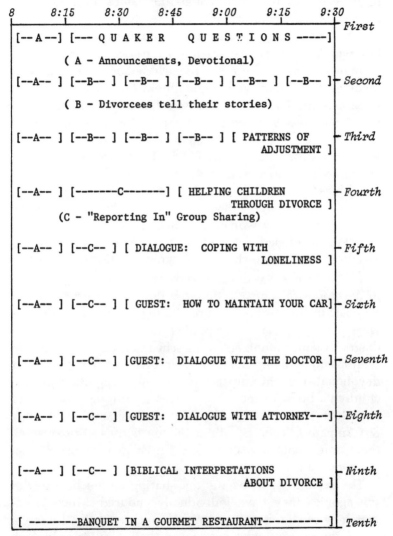

*Figure B.   Divorcee Care Groups: How The Ten Sessions
Are used.*

under way: *Don't!* Instead, collect the names until you have enough for a second group.

8. **We typed a list of telephone numbers for each woman to have.** At the very first session, we passed this list of each woman's telephone numbers to each person attending. This involved more than you might think, Fred. Most of them were *unlisted*. There was a trust relationship developed as the women received that slip of paper. It was a commitment to each other which had an element of protectiveness to it. And how those gals kept in TOUCH with one another! We encouraged them to call someone else in the group when the "blues" set in or when a crisis arose. It was deeply moving to get the reports in the beginning "small talk" each Monday evening about how women had helped one another.

9. **We developed a successful pattern for the ten weeks together.** Let me sketch out a diagram to illustrate it, Fred:

The first week was devoted to the use of Quaker Questions to develop a relationship between the women which would be basic to the deeper level of sharing. A review of the ten weeks was given at the beginning time (marked "A" in the diagram), and volunteers were scheduled for the next two sessions to tell the story of their divorces. For your first devotional, I might surprise you by my suggestion: read a children's book to them . . . pages 15 through the top of page 20 in *The Velveteen Rabbit* (Margery Williams, Doubleday & Company). You see, it's a bit too early to "broadside" the women with a distinctively Christian message. If you do, some will not return.

The second week begins the sharing of the histories of the agonies they have individually endured. Much cross-matching of stories will occur, as women remark, "I thought I was the *only one* who ever faced that!" Try to hold each person to 15 minutes. Plan on running over! For a devotion this night, you may want to read 1 Corinthians 13 from a modern version.

Session three will complete the story-telling times. You may use the balance of the time to review a section I'll give you in a moment describing the patterns of adjustment women in divorce may face. Let each person share as you go into their identification with these stages. For a devotional, select an appropriate passage from Oswald Chambers' *My Utmost for His Highest*. Use it for the rest of the devotionals. From the 365 he has written, you will find one that *just fits* each session. If you have a budget to use for such a purpose, it would be a great thing to give each woman a copy of this book at the last session.

With the fourth session, schedule a "Reporting In" time. Give each divorcee opportunity to share significant problems she is facing. These can lead into deep discussions! I shall never forget one group where a girl shared her fear that an affair with a man had left her pregnant. Suddenly, the significance of abortion was not abstract. We discussed the pros and cons of her situation for several hours.

This leads me to remind you, Fred, that the schedule suggested must not be followed rigidly. "Play it by ear." If the "Reporting In" is going to run over, let the women decide whether to go on with the scheduled subject for the next period, and come back to the issues at 9:30, or simply scrap the next subject and continue. When you have guest speakers, you will want to give them the time allotted, of course, but don't *kill* the sharing time without giving the chance for further discussion.

In the fourth session, let the women talk among themselves about how their children have handled the divorce of their parents. Your own preliminary reading will give you insights to share at this point, and your listening to these discussions will soon make you an "expert" on the various ways women handle the crises of the children.

Session five will also make use of your preliminary reading when you lead in a discussion of how divorcees cope with loneliness. Questions to get things started may include:

What is the most difficult day of the week for you?

What are the "booby traps" to watch out for in treating your loneliness?

What can you do about getting out of the house when your budget won't even allow an expenditure? (Art museum, zoo, window shopping, etc.)

Don't worry about how you'll fill *this* time! Worry about how you'll get them to go home *on* time. This is a subject that has great meaning for divorcees.

The next three sessions will utilize guests. Select them with care. First, find a Christian *mechanic* in your area who will be sympathetic to your project. Explain to him that most of the divorcees depended upon their husbands for the auto problems they had and are now unable to protect themselves from "vultures" who take advantage of them when they go in to have their car serviced. How can they know when something needs to be repaired? How to change a tire?—You may want to ask the women to meet in the garage that night and wear old clothes. This is a problem every woman needs help to solve.

Do you have a marriage counselor, a psychologist, or a psychiatrist who would give you one evening every twenty weeks or so? If so, let him come prepared to *answer questions,* not lecture. You can substitute a general practitioner of medicine if you do not have a counselor available. It may be valuable for the women to write their questions out in advance, give them to you in sealed envelopes, and let the doctor see them in advance. This provides anonymity for some who might be embarrassed to ask their question before the group. Questions about *why* their marriage went sour, *why* their husband's conduct is a certain way are among those usually asked. On one occasion, I substituted two mature divorced men for the doctor in this particular session and found it worked extremely well. The women wanted a "man's point of view" on their divorce problems, and a divorced man gave insights I never would have thought about.

When the attorney comes, you may be sure the questions will fly thick and fast. Alert the attorney that some in each group feel their own attorney is an *idiot*, and that the real problem is a fixation by a woman toward the lawyer, who has become the brunt of all her hostility and guilt over the divorce. It's usually better for the lawyer to know in advance who these women are and shrug off their barbs. In such situations, *no* defense of the attorney is going to change anything.

When it comes time to talk about biblical interpretations about divorce, you may or may not want to invite a clergyman. If you do, be sure he remains objective about the subject. I want to strongly suggest that *all* interpretations be objectively presented, from the Roman Catholic to the Jewish. Review all Scripture passages relating to the topic (there are not that many of them), and conclude by permitting each woman to struggle with the positions for herself. The matter of remarriage is often in their minds, of course, and no one is going to successfully dictate to another what should be done in this case. It must be a matter of personal conviction; and you, of course, have every right to share yours (for what it's worth). A number of excellent books are now on the market concerning this issue, and whoever does this presentation *must* do some research before sharing.

Throughout the ten weeks, pass a can around to collect a "kitty" for the final banquet. Let the women themselves decide how much they feel they want to spend for their individual meals, and give them ten weeks to "save up" enough for this big blowout. It does a great deal for a divorcee's morale to have an evening she otherwise would not be able to afford. (Ruth and I have often "sweetened the pot" without anyone knowing about it.) Schedule your table or room well in advance, and *go all out*. Long dresses are in order if it does not require additional expense for ladies with tight budgets.

After every one has been seated, ask each person to share what the group has meant to them. Also ask how the sessions can be improved. You might share information about continuing groups they may wish to join—hopefully, your own church will have a place for divorcees, other than a class of married women their age during Sunday School. Finally, give each person an opportunity to position themselves in their spiritual pilgrimage before the others. Suggest that some might want to become "helpers" in a new group being formed. One or two who have "graduated" from a group are extremely helpful in getting new groups off to a good start. Eventually, some of them will be leading groups all alone, as deeply committed Christians who have been called to their own TOUCH ministry.

Fred, here are some items you will face in working with divorcees, and some of the conclusions we came to about handling them:

1. *Unbiblical divorces.*—We never excused them; but there is a crucial difference between that and condemning a person who has been through one! A great deal of prayer, love, and common sense must mingle at this point.

2. *Financial problems.*—We always helped so anonymously that the woman never knew for sure who had assisted her. A drug bill at the pharmacy was just . . . *paid.* However, we never provided financial help for a woman's maintenance. If she is paying too much rent, driving a car she cannot afford, or dressing the children the way she did prior to the divorce, she does not need money: she needs instruction. We used money only for the crisis situations. Fortunately, our Deacon's Fund was open for us to use in meeting these needs.

3. *The footloose divorcee.*—Many a girl finds herself divorced in a city miles from all friends and relatives. Perhaps she and her husband were transferred there in connection with

a promotion in his company. Now cut off from him, she finds herself totally alone. In many situations like this, we have encouraged the woman to move back to her original town. Left alone, she will soon succumb to her rootless condition and often remarry thoughtlessly. It's a lot wiser to help her move close to her folks, a married sister, or close friends. This cannot always occur, but it is a good idea. Also, there are some situations where a move *away* from the town where her "ex" lives is the most valuable adjustment she can provide for her children. I recall an instance where an ex-husband would storm the apartment of his former wife in a drunken stupor and terrorize his grade-school children for hours on end. Court orders can go only so far in solving problems. Distance often solves more.

4. *Signs of anxiety.*—If the storm of divorce becomes too great, some women may crack. We have had this experience, too, Fred! Slashed wrists, mental breakdowns, and heavy use of pills can be replaced by love and concern through Divorcee Groups. Be alert to these possible symptoms: unusual weepiness, awaking in early hours of the morning, unkempt appearance, withdrawal from open sharing in the group.

5. *Lack of future plans.*—Long-range planning will do as much as anything to help divorcees get on the positive side of life. If possible, ask frequently, "What will you be doing five years from now? What should you be doing *now* to make those plans a reality?" I could tell you many stories about the women who have been challenged by that statement to make positive plans, instead of moping. Of all our divorcees, one of our favorites is now operating a successful beauty shop in a distant state because of the encouragement given in a group to make long-range plans.

Of greatest importance, of course, is . . .

HOW WE USED DIVORCEE GROUPS IN EVANGELISM

You have probably wondered, as you have listened to me

outline the schedule for the sessions, how we shared Christ with these dear women. Obviously, it did not occur in heavy doses in the sessions. This is quite intentional. We tried that approach and were saddened to lose some who were not willing to attend the group after it became "religious."

Our evangelism took place on the Monday nights when the group did *not* meet. This was a time for personal relationships. We visited the homes of the women, meeting their children and drinking coffee as we talked. From the group, we became familiar with the "hole in the heart" in each person. In the personal moments of sharing, we talked about the personal relationship to Christ each girl needed to have. This could be adapted to her needs, her background, her feelings of guilt about her divorce. Those who were "cool" to the gospel were carefully cultivated, prayed over, and patiently led to a point where a more meaningful TOUCH with Christ could be suggested.

We had many, many converts! Mothers and children gradually came into our fellowship, and several other congregations in the area were also blessed with those who were harvested by our groups. For us, however, the pattern of intimate sharing was on the personal level, not the group level. We considered it the "pre-evangelism point."

Holes in the heart which often gave us opportunity to win women included a feeling that their children were suffering terribly because of the divorce. Without a husband to help, a woman without Christ is in deep need of assistance . . . from Jesus! Another *hole* was the feeling that, because she could not "hold her man," she was less than a whole person. To help her realize that whatever her own failure might have been in connection with the marriage, there is an *abundant life* available in Christ and that is *Good News* indeed.

Children in the divorced home were also a potential for evangelism which required us to visit in the homes. Many times these youngsters had never been in church services and were unaware of Christ's love. By referring them to Rap Sessions, inviting them to go on youth retreats, we saw many commit themselves eventually to the Master.

What of the husbands? Yes, Fred, we have even had opportunity to witness to them! In these cases, I usually called the man at his office. I would say, "My wife and I have a Divorcee group meeting in our home, and your former wife has been attending. I asked her permission to call you . . . not for her sake, but for mine. I wonder if you would like to give me some insights into what caused the marriage to fail which might make it possible to minister more intelligently to her?" In a few rare instances this was the start of a long series of luncheons with the man and a chance to point him to Christ.

Before I get up to put another log on the fire, let me add this final word about . . .

STAGES DIVORCEES OFTEN PASS THROUGH ON THE ROAD TO WHOLENESS

We pegged down about eight of these over the months of sharing with the women. Not all divorcees go through all stages, nor in the order I have listed them. However, we have dealt with them all more than once.

1. The "No! It's Not True!" Stage

This is first: a rejection that the ugly ogre of divorce has really invaded the home. It is marked by fast swings of emotion . . . relief, bitterness, sadness, second thoughts, wondering why the marriage ever happened in the first place. It's *not* over, it *is* over. It's *good*, it's *horrible!* Women who have undergone hypnosis two years after their divorce still talk as though they were married . . . indicating that their subconscious mind has still not accepted the reality of the separation.

2. The "I'm Going to Try Again!" Stage

This is usually the point where I call the husband and

chat. She thinks maybe it will work. Often there may be
a flurry of dating again, even a weekend spent together. I
am sure a small percentage of couples return to marriage
again at this point, but we never saw it take place. Instead,
there was a return to the group with a comment like, "I
guess I had forgotten how impossible things had become
between us. We both realized there are no pieces to pick
up." However impossible it might sound to try it again, I
always encourage her to try. If anything *could* save a broken
marriage, it's worth the effort!

3. The "My Husband Is a Rat!" Stage

This can be precipitated by the children returning from
their weekend stay with Daddy with news about his girlfriend
who spent the night with them at the beach or by the news
that he has not paid his alimony on time . . . again! It is
important to try to temper this feeling for the sake of the
children. Paul Tournier's book, *To Understand Each Other*,
suggests that men who turn to other women prior to the
breakup of a marriage often do so because of an overdomi-
nant wife. Other valuable insights from the book may be useful
in helping a woman be more objective about her ex-husband.
And of course, there are *plenty* of situations where the husband *is* a rat! Sometimes it is hard to remain objective.

Another side to this coin is where Mama herself is a rat.
Sometimes her sowing of adulterous seed prior to the breakup
has left her vulnerable, and she patiently waits for some signs
from the husband of similar behavior to use as a self-jus-
tification. Sin is sin! There are some delicate tight-ropes to
be walked when working in this area. It takes a lot of praying
for wisdom, and a great deal of patience to know how to
say the right things.

4. The "All Men Are Rats!" Stage

This usually is coupled with the first month at the office
as a secretary after years of being a housewife. Word travels
quickly through the sales staff about the cute divorcee up

on the second floor. Married men come up to sympathize and commiserate about their *own* unhappy marriage, making not-so-veiled hints that they would *love* to become a "part-time husband" if she feels the urge for a shoulder to lean on. Along with it, there may be the beginnings of . . .

5. The "How Do I Handle Sex Now?" Stage

It's a lot better to bring this out in the open than to hope it will go away! It's really a problem and needs to be faced squarely. Some women handle it by suddenly gaining 25 pounds to make themselves unattractive. Others I have known break patterns of a lifetime and "slip away" to bars, fantasizing the fun of being picked up. When it actually happens, they are shocked at themselves and usually spend weeks of self-loathing afterwards. It's just not worth it!

6. The "How Do I Handle My Children?" Stage

Adolescent boys are a special problem. So is the Monday after good old Dad has had the kids for the weekend, has spent gobs of money on them, spoiled them rotten, and then returned them to Mom . . . who is trying to get along on the meager salary as a secretary and hardly has enough extra to buy ice cream. How does she make a five-year old understand why *she* can't "have fun with them like Daddy does"? In a dozen other ways, despair over the children faces the mother. In one situation, a child was so torn up by the divorce of the parents that he pulled his hair out . . . one strand at a time! In another, the child deliberately stole from a store in full view of the manager, hoping that his arrest would make his daddy pay some attention to him.

7. The "When Will I Remarry?" Stage

This is closely coupled with the questions about what the Bible teaches about remarriage. Fred, I have never fully understood this, but even unbelieving divorcees in our country have an avid interest in what the Scriptures say about the rights of a divorced person to remarry. For myself, it is obvious that Scripture *does* permit this in certain circumstances. But beyond this, there is the question of how long one should wait, how does one insure the *next* one will not go sour, and similar problem areas. These are best dealt with on an individual basis.

8. The "Settling In" Stage

Those who make a satisfactory adjustment to their divorced state are the women who eventually set long-range goals and begin the journey toward them. The purchase of a house by a certain date; the completion of college; the opening of a business; the education of the children . . . the possibilities for these goals are too numerous to list! The eventual possibility of remarriage is settled—one way or the other—but no longer becomes a pressing issue to be solved, regardless of compromises with reality. Women who are in this stage are of the greatest possible assistance in launching additional groups. When they are also deeply committed Christians, they make the very *finest* leaders for Divorcee TOUCH Groups.

They're all around you, Fred! People in crisis, people in change. People waiting for us to TOUCH them in Christ's name. I don't fully understand why the churches of today seem so embarrassed to face the reality of the divorced in the world about them. In the United States, they are without a doubt the largest Target Group of all . . . and the most open for ministry and evangelism. I pray that a year from now your Body will have a dozen groups going!

---

[1] See Roger Crook, *An Open Book to the Christian Divorcee* (Nashville: Broadman Press, 1974).

13

F.L.O.C.: A Healing TOUCH
for Bleeding Parents

Once upon a starry night, a beautiful woman wrote a poem which summarized her recent life:

> I had a child.
> God gave him to me.
> *He wasn't perfect, and he wasn't like me!*
> All the things I thought he should be
>   were like the wind that eluded me.
> I wished for the moon and the end of my grief,
> But God saw, and provided
> His Blessed Relief.

This mother's life has been transformed twice. The first time was when she gave birth to an "exceptional" child; the second time was when the indwelling Christ was born into her.

If it had not been for Bill and Betty's F.L.O.C. ministry, she quite possibly would still be longing for the "end of her grief!" Fred, the FLOC name was "borrowed" from the Church of the Savior in Washington, D.C. It stands for: For the Love Of Children. It seemed to be the perfect word to describe our ministry to parents of exceptional children.

We all have known rejection at some point in our life. For some of us, it may have occurred during childhood when a play group chose to ostracize us. For others, it occurred during adolescence when our "steady" decided to go out with someone else. *Remember how painful it was?*

Many couples in our community feel a much deeper rejection. They exist in a shell of emotional hurt, resulting from a circumstance that is no fault of their own.

They became parents of exceptional children. Born retarded, autistic, mentally or emotionally disturbed, disabled, each child is in some way . . . *handicapped.* These parents share a common emotion: dejection. They also share a common fate: rejection. FLOC can help remedy both the emotion and the fate.

Parents who are in this dilemma are in need of much understanding. They need as much care and love as the youngster they look after. Government and medical services provide assistance for children. FLOC ministers to the moms and dads. They live with their problem, knowing what their child will never know: the difference between being "normal" and "exceptional."

Many uninformed persons feel that a handicapped child might somehow "contaminate" their own normal child if they were allowed to come into contact with each other. Such neanderthal thinking is particularly strong against children who are retarded, mentally or emotionally disturbed, or autistic. It is an unfortunate truth that the churches of many communities are among those who have left the deepest scars of rejection upon the parents of special children. I have heard parents in our FLOC group tell of rejections by local churches that would make a marble statue weep with embarrassment!

People are usually afraid of what they do not understand, Fred. For this reason when we launched our FLOC ministry, we prepared our folks in the church for the eventual ingathering of families who would be reached for Christ. We had parents show slides of their children, explaining the precise situation, and telling our members how to relate to them in the halls and in the services. We provided special classes when this would be best for the child, and placed them in regular classes when this would be most valuable.

Got any parents of such children in your fellowship? Tell them about our own Bill and Betty. Their very intimate knowledge of the needs of such parents was learned through the coming of a precious girl God placed in their home. For many months, she attended a special institution. When she was about six, she came to live at home. You name *any* problem parents of exceptional children have: Bill and Betty have faced them. Most beautiful of all, their story includes the entrance of Christ into their home. From that time, a spiritual growth within them reflected itself in their dear child. Unbelievable progress has been made by her.

Such a couple may be instrumental in helping a FLOC group begin in your neighborhood, too! Let me encourage them by telling you this: No other TOUCH ministry has produced as many converts as FLOC has in its three-year history. I am amazed as I recall also how the TOUCH ministries have related to FLOC. The HOPE ministry has referred several International couples to FLOC. It, too, became "missionary" in that sense.

Discovering parents of exceptional children will not be hard. There is a close network established between them in connection with the medication, therapy, and education of their children. Notices placed in the establishments where such help is given will get preliminary word around that FLOC is starting. Local chapters of national groups may be listed in your telephone directory.

These organizations will be happy to put others in touch with you. They are anxious to provide all the possible assistance to parents who are looking for help.

FLOC is for adults. It provides a forum for sharing hurts, rejections, fears, angers, *and solutions.* They may do so, confident that every one in the room will understand their feelings. In this forum, the peace of Jesus Christ in the lives of the couple who have found him to be sufficient will be obvious. Through this TOUCH of the Spirit, many have received the Lord who has "been tested in all points" with us.

Bill and Betty found Thursday night was as good an evening as any for their FLOC group. Bill converted their garage into a playroom, and trained workers cared for the children while parents met in the den. Informality marked the sessions. Dress was informal. Plenty of coffee and pastries brought by women on a volunteer basis were readily available.

The format for the Divorcee ministry can serve as a pattern for FLOC as well. Opening remarks and a devotional, followed in the early weeks by nothing but time for each person or couple to tell their story, is pretty much the format. Unlike the Divorcee group, however, keep membership open. From time to time, the group may agree to an invitation being extended to a doctor, psychiatrist, or therapist who can speak to a topic of mutual interest. However, the most important thing is to keep the status of a *forum*, where anyone who is hurting can get the floor.

After a few weeks, it became obvious that FLOC would profit from having a "silent chair" in the den. This was simply a tweed-covered chair that was designated for a dad or mom who felt a need to be in the group, but who was too torn up inside to enter into conversation. It was often used!

Once a quarter, the group shared a common meal—"pot luck." Folding tables were squeezed into every available space in the home. Thanksgiving dinners were also shared by this group. Twice a year our TOUCH Ranch was used by the group. The entire families would spend a weekend together there with special events for the children who were exceptional as well as for the other normal children. Baby-sitters were hired to give parents a "break" to do some things together.

News media will be glad to do features on the FLOC ministry. Be sure to get permission before allowing a photographer to take pictures. Word stories will help spread the word about the activities and attract new people. However, keep the meetings themselves "closed." Occasions are rare where parents can be totally transparent about their feelings.

They need no observers to inhibit honest reactions.

Husbands will profit from an evening scheduled for a discussion of the financial hardships caused by providing for the special needs of their child. Another evening might be devoted to a discussion of how other couples handle their social life with an exceptional child living in the home. Notes about medications and therapies will be compared and many helpful suggestions given to newcomers in the community.

Opportunity will present itself early in the sessions for the host and hostess to share their faith in Jesus Christ. Because so many couples have felt rejection by churches, it may be expected that some will respond with anger or cynicism to their honest report of commitment to Christ. If this is anticipated, the Christian couple will realize that the verbal testimony must be followed by a *consistent silent witness.* They will know the "breakthrough" has come when the telephone begins to ring through the week and members of the group begin to pour out their concerns.

Gradually, couple by couple, the awareness will come that the sponsors of FLOC consider their relationship to Christ to be as important a help to their child as the advice of the doctors. The inner peace displayed on a consistent basis before the group will eventually attract them to Christ.

Fred, as pastor of West Memorial I have been invited to FLOC about twice a year to speak on the subject, "Why, God?" I don't think I have worked as hard on any message in my life as that one . . . and I improved it with each repeat. As God's man, I was expected to help those parents comprehend why God would do such a thing to *them* and *their* child! I found help for myself in a multitude of places, including Dale Evans Rogers' book *Angel Unaware* and Norman Grubb's book, *The Spontaneous You.*

I recall Bill mentioning with pride to me one day that since FLOC had started, Betty had become a "part-time housewife." Those two were "on call" 24 hours a day, available to listen, to advise, to visit couples or individuals in the group who had special needs. Again, as with the Divorcee group, most of the evangelism was *personal* evangelism. One by one, parents came to know Christ. There followed some cautious steps testing the thickness of love among the members at West Memorial. After we "passed the test" as a congregation, our FLOC folks began to put their *full* weight down on us. Sunday after Sunday, I would look out over our worship service and spot FLOC couples. It always made my heart glad.

Betty shared this story with me: "I recall one young woman who had three children, one with very serious problems. As a result of the conflict caused by this child, her husband left her. She came to the end of herself, not knowing what to do. FLOC became a regular part of her week. After several months, she called me on the telephone one day, weeping bitterly. She said, 'I just can't take it any more! I can't go on!' I simply shared with her how she could put her life—and children—into the care of Jesus Christ. Alone in her home, she accepted the Lord talking to me on the telephone."

Twenty-one couples were active in FLOC at last count, Fred. These are couples being reached by *one* couple who discovered that, for them, the exceptional child God gave them was the open door to one of the most productive target groups in our society!

14

S.T.I.T.C.H.:
Needle and TOUCH for Women

Fred, this week's TOUCH News is over there on the end table. Take a look at the reports of TOUCH ministries in it . . . the right-hand column . . . see them? Notice that one group is called S.T.I.T.C.H.—and that they had twenty-five women present last week!

You guessed it: *that's a sewing group.* The letters stand for *Sewing Together In The Christian Home.* There is a fellowship among women with needles in their hands which goes as far back as Eve and her daughters. Women naturally talk with needles in their hands. *(No more remarks from the kitchen, Ruthie!)*

Joyce is just about the greatest seamstress that ever came out of East Texas, and her special gifts of the Spirit and skills of the fingers were brought together to shape this target-group ministry. Her reputation in the neighborhood had gone before her, and women were delighted to get help from such an expert . . . *free.* These morning sessions start after the kids are packed off to school and households have been straightened up. Then the cars begin to gather in front of her house, and women carrying material and salad bowls come streaming in the door. Tatting, quilting, crocheting, dressmaking—you name it, and there will be some woman doing it in STITCH. Nearby each Outsider, there will be a Christian gal who is sharing in the womanly "small talk" in a normal way. When the time is right, the talk turns to matters of faith. Concepts are shared back and forth. Women who are responsive to the simple testimonies of faith that are shared are cultivated in the most practical ways in the days which follow.

At noon, seams are pinned, fabric is returned to cardboard boxes, and women gather to eat the salad buffet they have all helped to prepare. *More small talk!* More awarenesses provided to loving Christian women of a mother worried about a son, a wife concerned about her husband, a lady thinking deeply about her spiritual laxness.

Small talk almost always leads to deep conversations. Sometimes they can take place in STITCH, sometimes over a very personal cup of coffee the next morning with a trusted friend who drops by for a few minutes.

The pattern never varies, except for the area of interest of the target group. First, the TOUCH. Then, the awareness of the holes in the hearts of Outsiders. Next, the sharing of Christ's salvation in a very specific way which reaches through the *hole* . . . to the *heart.* The rest is up to the Holy Spirit, who has been sent to guide Outsiders to Jesus. The thrilling thing about this Target-Group Evangelism is that it works. It reaches people. It means that every single Christian can have a very personal ministry. Each TOUCH worker develops a special relationship with no more than five people: remember . . . that's about all a person with normal responsibilities in life can effectively minister to, if time is to remain for work, family, and worship experiences.

STITCH is a way that quiet, shy Christian ladies can share their faith without feeling uncomfortable. It is also a way that women can first be TOUCHed for Bible study groups. As in many other of these ministries, the ten-week period in one group can lead to Bible study with those who are genuinely interested in knowing more about Christ.

There is a precious fellowship among Christians who become involved in TOUCH groups. There is probably less spirit of rivalry and competition here, less duplication of efforts here, than in any other missionary activity in the world. Their tasks are to sow, cultivate, weed, and eventually, harvest. God gives the increase.

Sometimes their task is to STITCH. Needling and threading their way into the fabric of human lives which have been cut and torn is a serious matter. It has a tendency to wear out the skin on the knees!

15

What's Next?

Once the mentality of Christians is developed to see the world of Outsiders as *groups,* the potential for evangelism becomes one huge explosion of ministries. They must be discovered by those who will leave the buildings of religion long enough to see the real live world around us.

Gradually, ever so gradually, we are drifting toward this concept of evangelism. A special ministry to those who work in the race track world has led to Race Track Chaplains being established. A friend of mine is patiently trying to crack the armor plate of a major oil company, ready to minister to their top-level employees. His thesis is solid: it's a lot wiser to lose men to *faith* than to *liquor!* A large group of VIP's every year are washed out by whiskey.

A network of Christians is currently springing up around the world to minister to men who have gone down to the sea in ships. They are discovering that every seaport is a *world mission field.*

Thousands of men roam the highways of this nation hauling freight in semitrucks. Someone began to see the opportunity to reach these nomadic drivers. There is a little newspaper now printed to distribute to them. Another target group entered for Christ!

I have not even exhausted the target groups we discovered and worked with at West Memorial, Fred! There are several more. Each month someone else gets another vision of loving, and another group is born. Sometimes a TOUCH ministry attracts little attention to itself, since it is the result of one person gathering his five and ministering to them. Since no budget is needed, it comes to the attention of no special committee. Since there presently exists no denominational "report system" to share these exciting results, these un-recognized evangels catch each other in hallways and report to each other. Often they end up praying together. Sometimes they end up pooling their money to TOUCH someone who has a special need.

I keep remembering the story of a man I worked with a few years ago who is one of God's dear preachers today. He used to run a beer hall . . . a couple of them, to be exact! All the political fuss about banning alcohol made by the churches in his state would not have drawn him one inch closer to heaven. It took a warm smile and a strong handshake from a real, live Christian who walked into his beer joint one day to shut him down forever! After Christ entered his life, he told me he took the keys to his joint, with slot machines in the back room, and pitched them into the piney woods. Hurrah for a man who, like Jesus, became a friend of winebibbers and sinners.

Fred, I also keep remembering the story of the first prosti-tute I ever got to know in a deeply personal way. She was strung out on heroin, filled with self-loathing, and hurting so badly for a TOUCH of Jesus that it broke my heart. I'll never forget the night she walked forward at West Memorial, weeping bitterly. She literally *soaked* the shoulder of my coat with hot tears and black mascara. For thirteen years she had lived in a group which had *never* become the target for evan-gelism. She was living in hell and also in sight of church spires all over her city. *Why* do we not move with anguished hearts to the brothels, the bars, of our cities? What are we waiting for?

What about firemen, with hours to play poker and watch television in their fire houses? What of ticket takers in theaters? What about bulldozer operators, gathered at the local pub for a "short one" on the way home? What of the

factory workers?

In Houston one dark night, my son Ralph and I donned TOUCH jackets and took off to relate to teenage dopers. At that time, one of the places drugs were pushed fast and furiously was an all-night doughnut shop. We went in, ordered coffee, and sat back to "case the joint" before beginning to witness. I was impressed by the activity of the woman behind the counter. She was middle-aged, intelligent, and knew many of the youths by name. She also became, as I observed her, an *obvious Christian.* It wasn't that she "preached" to anyone, but the words she said to young girls and freaked-out long hairs penetrated deeply.

When the crowd thinned out, I went over and introduced myself. I said, "You're one of the Body, aren't you?" With shining eyes she replied, "Yup. Sure am." I also discovered in the conversation which followed what *else* she was: a graduate of a Bible institute, a missionary who had returned to the States because of ill health, *and a women who knew a mission field when she saw one.* Hundreds of Christians in that area "stayed away" from that doughnut shop; she got a job working all night in it! The fact that she worked for a pittance did not bother her missionary heart one bit. Nor did the crazy 10 P.M. to 6 A.M. schedule make her hesitate. She had jockeyed herself into a position where she could do eight hours a night, six nights a week, what son Ralph and I could do as customers for only an hour or so. Her relationships with those youngsters were deep. They trusted her implicitly. Eventually many of them trusted the Christ she recommended.

Fred, God gave each of us gifts so that we might minister. When we see the diversity of those gifts, and the enormity of the opportunities, we can only ask: "Lord, What's Next?"

16

Epilogue

During the next twenty-five years, the destiny of thousands of people will be determined by how many more pages men like you, Fred, will add to your notes. You are aware that Genesis is "The Book of Beginnings," aren't you? I'd like to write those words across the front of your tablet. I pray you will add many more pages, as ministries are shaped by the needs of Outsiders in your town.

In Miami's suburbs a dear widower drove me from a church to my lodging place following a dialogue about TOUCH ministries with the congregation. He told me about his lonely eighteen months without his precious wife. With deep emotion, he said: "You know, until now I never really knew how to relate to people who had lost their mates. Now I know!" At fifty-six years of age his eyes were opened to a new target group: *the widowers.* He is now in a unique position to become related to them through a TOUCH ministry of his own.

As life flows, there are constant streams of situations which trigger awarenesses of new target groups. Parents who have gone through the trauma of uncovering evidence of drug use by their own child know in a *special* way how the blood drains to the ankles at such a moment. Hundreds of others have *also* wished at such a time for somewhere to go for help. Who will TOUCH them with Christ's redemptive love?

As long as we care, we will find people to care for . . . and new ways to relate the gospel of Jesus Christ to those who turn away from the traditional church we know today. The potential for evangelism is endless!

Fred, before you go I want to challenge you to join me in concern about a situation that has quietly developed in our nation which makes target-group evangelism a matter of urgency. I refer to the *process of urbanization.*

Did you know that at the end of the next quarter of a century, more people will be living in the major cities of the earth than are now living *on* the earth? It's a fact!

Evangelism as we now know it is rooted in the soil of a rural way of life. I was surprised to discover that in one major denomination, 30,129 out of 34,665 churches are located in open country, villages, and towns of less than 50,000 population. According to *The Quarterly Review: A Survey of Southern Baptist Progress* (Vol. 34, No. 4, p. 7) only 4,536 of the total are situated in the massive urban centers of the nation!

Our country background has influenced our mentality more than we want to admit. But unless we *do* admit it, we will not wake up in time to reach a full generation of Outsiders for Christ. Target-group evangelism is the method of the world that is fast becoming urban.

Anthropologists explain that the migration of people from country to city breaks up all patterns of life. The words "tribal group" refer just as effectively to people in Pine Mountain, Georgia, as to the people in Chichicastenango, Guatemala. To grow up in an area where everyone knows everyone else intimately, where intermarriage has occurred for generations, is *not* the exclusive property of "natives" living in foreign lands.

In the small village, Mr. Smith at the hardware store knows Jim, his family, and his family tree—going back thirty years. In such a setting, "people do for each other." In such a culture, people have religion, and they aren't *about* to change it, thank you! *It's tied to family.*

As in Guatemala, so in Georgia: a migration by a family to the city (Atlanta, for instance) is a traumatic experience.

The hardware store has become a monstrous Handy Dan, with aisles of items impersonally stacked and a stranger at the checkout counter. The apartment complex is run by a racy-looking blonde who just does not seem to be the type one complains to about the neighbors on the left who fight half the night, or the ones on the right who throw wild "pot" parties.

All previous relationships have been destroyed by the violent contrasts between rural and urban cultures. For a large majority of the migrants, religion is tied to the family back home. In the city, the little church of the village (with doors *never* locked) has become a huge building with a massive staff, locked doors, and surface smiles.

Those who have analyzed the patterns of adjustment from rural to urban indicate that people's lives are "up for grabs" during the first few months in their new environment. Those of no religion are now open to one. Those of "back home" religion may easily drift to secularism.

Why not test this thesis out in a housing development in a city of your choice? Knock on any 50 doors in a row, and ask the people about these matters. You'll observe these facts for yourself! In a larger number than you may expect, you will find people who never attend church who never missed, "down home." And you will also find those involved in eastern religions and cults who *used* to be members of "old line" denominations, B.C. (Before City).

TOUCH ministries can infiltrate a community, relating to people during this period of social upheaval. An interior decorating class would be a possibility here, offering help to young couples in fixing up an apartment on a limited budget. There *are* ways of "snagging" people who are open to new ways for new days. But there is a limit to the period of time when this can occur.

In a few short months—at best, a year—the new, urban pattern has become structured in the lives of migrants from villages. By then, they will have either related to Christ or perhaps to a lake and a boat, with weekends without God. When this secular arrangement is adopted, Christians may well watch (with sinking hearts) for *years* as a family rears its children apart from knowledge of Christ's lordship. Perhaps a crisis of overwhelming dimensions will occur to this family; then they will be shaken hard enough for another TOUCH to reach them.

With the present rapid pattern of urbanization in the nation, the urgency of breaking out of the old molds is too great to be put into words! Fred, IT'S NOW OR NEVER. If we ever intend to move into the lives of people, it must be *now*.

The trend towards repeating the past is very strong. It is much easier to recycle what we did last year than to venture into new areas of outreach. This inertia must be overcome! This pattern is as evident in the structures of the church as it is in other areas of society. My friend T. Frank Hardesty, one of the most colorful lecturers on management I have ever met, recites this poem to make the point:

THE CALF PATH

One day, through the primeval wood
A calf walked home, as good calves should
But made a trail all bent askew
A crooked trail, as all calves do.

That trail was taken up next day
By a dog that passed that way
And then a wise bellwether sheep
Pursued the trail o'er vale and steep
And drew the flock behind him, too
As good bellwethers always do.

And from that day, o'er hill and glade
Through those old woods a path was made
And many *men* wound in and out

And dodged, and turned, and bent about
And uttered words of righteous wrath
Because 'twas such a crooked path
But still they followed . . . do not laugh . . .
The first migrations of that calf.

The years passed on in swiftness fleet
The road became a village street
And this, before men were aware
A city's crowded thorofare.

Each day a hundred thousand rout
Trailed that zigzag calf about
And o'er his crooked journey went
The traffic of a continent.
A hundred thousand men were led
By one calf near two centuries dead.

A moral lesson this might teach
Were I ordained and called to preach
For *men* are prone to go it blind
Along the calf-paths of the mind
They work away from sun to sun
To do what *other* men have done
They follow in the beaten track
And out and in and forth and back
And *still* their devious course pursue
To keep the path that others do.

But how the wise old wood-gods laugh
Who saw that first primeval calf!

—Author unknown

Will we go on as before, repeating the patterns of an outdated, rural society church structure in the urban explosion all around us? Will we make the break soon enough to reach the present cities of our nation? Evangelism must take on urban dimensions to relate the good news of salvation in Jesus Christ to as many people as possible, in as many ways as possible.

Whether we win that race against time will depend not only upon changes introduced by men in places of influence in shaping church structures, but also upon the laity, Fred. Will *you* wait for someone else to "do it first"? Will you play it safe, waiting for the "trend" to be established? Will you delay until a full "curriculum" is ready to be ordered, and for a new staff member to be added to the inventory of specialists?

I pray you will TOUCH lives *now!* Fields white unto harvest are all around you. Call them . . . *Target Groups.*

Fred drove away from the house which had become a "one-day seminary in evangelism" for him, deep in thought. As he entered the freeway, he was conscious in a new way of the thousands of people living on either side of that concrete strip. Apartments, subdivisions whizzed by. His mind was also racing. New ways to win people? Not really. Just a stronger emphasis upon something we could have been doing all along. As he thought of all the personalities represented in his own community, he thought of how he should share these concepts with other members of his congregation. How? "Ver-r-r-y qui-i-i-ckly!" He said aloud, "Ver-r-r-y qui-i-i-ckly!"

Good trip, Fred. Keep in TOUCH!

Appendix

Suggested Schedule for Introducing Target Groups to a Church

Four Months in Advance: Schedule Lay Renewal Weekend to launch Journey Inward. For Preparation Manual, write to Director, Lay Renewal, 1548 Poplar Avenue, Memphis, Tennessee 38104

PHASE I: THE JOURNEY INWARD

First Quarter Theme: The Growth
1. Launch the Journey Inward with the "Lay Renewal Weekend."
2. Begin Journey Groups, meeting weekly. Use David Haney's *Journey Into Life* as the guide for groups. (Available at Baptist Book Stores. Published by Brotherhood Commission, SBC)
3. Conduct a retreat for all Journey Groups at end of second month. Use I AM CRUCIFIED booklets, tapes, and transparencies. (Available from Evangelism Research Foundation, Box 42360, Houston, Texas 77042. Also request Catalog describing pins, jackets, tapes, etc.)
4. Schedule "Renewal Evangelism Weekend" to launch Journey Outward. For Preparation Manual, write to Director, Lay Renewal, Brotherhood Commission, (address above, or to Renewal Evangelism, Home Mission Board, SBC, 1350 Spring St., N.W., Atlanta, Ga. 30309.

Second Quarter Theme: The Gifts
1. Continue Journey Groups, using *This Gift Is Mine* Kits. (Available at religious bookstores. Published by Broadman Press.)
2. Initiate a self-study of David Haney's *Renew My Church* (Zondervan, 1972) for each member of Journey Groups. This should be completed before the end of the second month.
3. Conduct a "mini-retreat" for all Journey Groups at end of second month (Supper, through 10 P.M. closing time). Use "Small Group Creative Procedures" for chapters 3, 5, and 7 in *Renew My Church.*

'$_2\$7$,
$\frac{9}{7}19$

PHASE II: THE JOURNEY OUTWARD

Third Quarter Theme: The Gap

1. Launch the Journey Outward with the "Renewal Evangelism Weekend."
2. Continue Journey Groups, using Ralph W. Neighbour's *Journey Into Discipleship* as the guide for groups. (Available at Baptist Book Stores. Published by Brotherhood Commission, SBC)
3. Members of Journey Groups initiate a self-study of *The TOUCH of the Spirit* (Broadman, 1972).
4. Conduct a "mini-prayer retreat" for all Journey Groups at end of second month. Use "Small Group Creative Procedures" for chapter 7 in *Renew My Church.*

Fourth Quarter Theme: The Group

1. Continue Journey Groups, using TOUCH Basic Training Course. (Available from Evangelism Research Foundation: 48-page workbook, tapes, transparencies, address above.)
2. Members of Journey Groups initiate a self-study of William Bangham's *Journey Into Small Groups.* (Available at Baptist Book Stores. Published by Brotherhood Commission, SBC)
3. Conduct a "mini-workshop" for all Journey Groups at end of second month. Use *Journey Into Small Groups* as guide for creative activities.
4. Launch Journey groups into TOUCH ministries to specific target groups.

REMEMBER . . . you will be the same person you now are in five years, **except** *for the people you meet and the books you read! This schedule is structured on the conviction that* **time** *is an essential ingredient in bringing about major change in life-styles of people. The weekly Journey Group meetings will accomplish much to structure time for the TOUCH ministries which follow.*